practical CLASSICS

& Car Restorer
ON
MIDGET/SPRITE
RESTORATION

Reprint from
Practical Classics magazine

ISBN 0 948 207 48 5

Published by
Brooklands Books with the permission of Practical Classics

Printed in Hong Kong

practical CLASSICS

Titles in this series

PRACTICAL CLASSICS ON AUSTIN A40 RESTORATION
PRACTICAL CLASSICS ON LAND ROVER RESTORATION
PRACTICAL CLASSICS ON METALWORKING IN RESTORATION
PRACTICAL CLASSICS ON MIDGET/SPRITE RESTORATION
PRACTICAL CLASSICS ON MINI COOPER RESTORATION
PRACTICAL CLASSICS ON MGB RESTORATION
PRACTICAL CLASSICS ON MORRIS MINOR RESTORATION
PRACTICAL CLASSICS ON SUNBEAM RAPIER RESTORATION
PRACTICAL CLASSICS ON TRIUMPH HERALD/VITESSE
PRACTICAL CLASSICS ON TRIUMPH SPITFIRE RESTORATION
PRACTICAL CLASSICS ON VW BEETLE RESTORATION
PRACTICAL CLASSICS ON 1930S CAR RESTORATION

Distributed by:

Brooklands Book Distribution Ltd.,
Holmerise, Seven Hills Road,
Cobham, Surrey KT11 1ES,
England.   Tel: 09326 5051

Motorbooks International,
Osceola,
Wisconsin 54020 U.S.A.
Tel: 715 294 3345

practical CLASSICS

CONTENTS

INTRODUCTION

We enjoyed our term with the Midget, the sixth car we have completely rebuilt in front of the camera for our 'Project Car' series. But this did not mean that the task of returning it to near-new condition was always easy — as with most old cars once you begin to strip the paint and remove other people's bodges, our Midget turned out to be rather more rusty than we had anticipated.

However, Ken Wright and Dave Jones who did the vast majority of panelwork in Lindsay Porter's workshop were not dismayed and the car emerged at the end with probably a better panel-fit than when it was new (in fact we *almost* forgive you, Ken and Lindsay, for trying to fit an MGB grille at one stage; every rebuild has its incident of brain-fade . . .).

Our thanks also go to our suppliers Spridgebits of Birmingham; Graham Sykes and Jed Watts really did pull out all the stops in finding all the parts for the car, from 'gold dust' items like a brand new front grille to the smallest nut and bolt. Their extensive range of second-hand spares were extremely useful too. Certainly, to attempt any work on a Spridget without their informative (and exhaustive) catalogue to hand amounts to sheer folly!

But we must also thank other suppliers and indeed it is one of the benefits of being a Spridget owner that there are now several reputable and efficient specialists serving this part of the MG market; certainly the Sprite and Midget Centre of Richmond, Surrey could not have been more helpful when the car was moved to Beckenham for its engine installation. Mentioning which, our thanks also goes to Eric Gilbert who made a superb job of rebuilding the engine, and who successfully tackled the 101 little detail finishing jobs which have to be done before a total restoration project finally wins an MoT certificate.

We were genuinely sad when it came to part with the Midget; it went in September 1985 to Mr Rolls who operates a garage near Maidenhead, Berks and who appreciated that here was a car into which had gone some 1,300 hours of work and almost exactly £3,000-worth of parts. We hope the Midget gives him good service; it certainly should do!

Introducing Our Spridget Rebuild/1

It didn't take us long to decide which sports car we should adopt to succeed our MGB project car. The MG Midget and its Sprite twin are, in our opinion, tremendous 'fun' cars offering very characterful motoring but with very modest running costs — and with, of course, a real fold-down hood, something that British motor manufacturers today are rapidly forgetting all about. One day Spridgets are going to emulate the original Frogeye Sprite (an example of which we restored in 1981) and become rather expensive to buy, but at the moment you pay little more than you would for a similarly-engined saloon of the same age and condition. condition.

So a Midget (or the mechnically identical Sprite, introduced as well in May 1961) is a near-ideal enthusiast's car, especially if you haven't an unlimited budget. Ours is a mid-1969 example, fitted with the larger, 1275cc version of the famous A-series engine which supplanted the 1098cc unit with the coming of the Mk III Midget in October 1966. It just pre-dates the 'face-lifted' versions of the Sprite and Midget which arrived in October 1969, these sporting Rostyle wheels, split rear bumper, and matt-black grille and sills.

You could say, therefore, that our car is the last of the 'traditional' Spridgets with its full-width bumpers and lack of modern touches such as the Rostyle wheels and the application of matt black everywhere; it has the optional wire wheels to continue the 'traditional' theme further still, though wires could also be specified on the later Spridgets which were mechanically identical (for practical purposes) until the introduction of the 1500 Triumph-engined, black-bumpered models in December 1974. The last of the series left the factory in April 1980, and were never replaced by an

'As found' — or at least, as acquired by Spridgebits on our behalf; a rather sorry-looking 1969 Midget, but lacking signs of drastic mods or bodging. Examples like this can still be bought for between £100 and £250.

Continued

Cheap and cheerful, and in the best traditions of the small British sports car — that's our latest Project Car. Paul Skilleter sets the scene.

Spridget Rebuild

Outer sills, bottom of front wing and scuttle all possess the typical rust-bubbles to be expected on elderly Spridgets.

A few gentle taps soon revealed considerable rear wheel arch rot beneath the filler!

An early look should always be taken at the lower hinge mounting on Sprites and Midgets — the pillar can be badly affected by rot here, and ours certainly is.

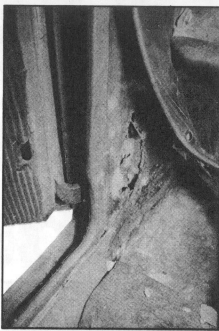

Looking behind the trim panel gives another view of the hinge pillar problem area.

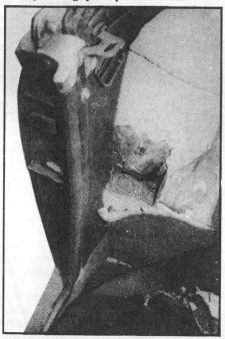

Serious rot here, in the bulkhead behind the seats, can mean writing-off the bodyshell; we reckon ours is repairable though. You have to pull back the trim to get a proper look here.

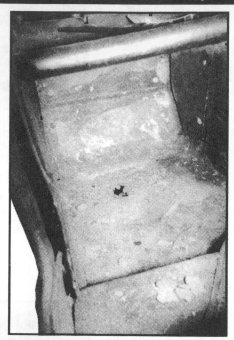

Footwells can be relied upon to rust and most passengers in old Spridgets end up with wet feet sooner or later!

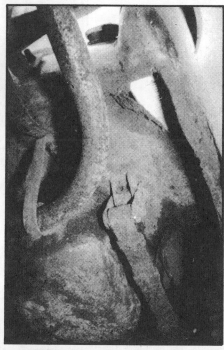

A view looking up from underneath of the rear spring hanger — this looks fairly sound but note big hole in boot floor top right!

equivalent model.

In choosing which type of Midget to buy we had the assistance of Spridgetbits, the well-known Sprite and Midget parts suppliers who operate from Birmingham and Redditch; Graham Sykes (who started the firm with partner Jed Watts in 1973) then proceeded to find us a 'suitable' example from the many which pass through the company's hands or which they get to hear about. Of course, as regular readers know, a car intended as a *Practical Classics* 'project' is not everyone's idea of 'suitable'! — but then there would be no point in us restoring a good example, would there?

Not that we wanted a total wreck — as with anyone looking for a good restoration prospect, ideally we needed a car that had a salvageable bodyshell and that — above all — was basically original and unmutilated; and this car represents almost exactly that, with the additional and important requirement that it was capable of being road-tested. This last is an advantage not to be under-esti-

Front spring hanger mounts on bulkhead and is an important safety point; note gaping holes in bottom of the box sections which make up this area.

Like most other cars, Spridget doors rot at the bottom of the skin . . .

. . . not to mention along the lower part of the door frame itself.

Don't forget the bonnet — this can suffer along the leading edges. While you're there, peep inside the grille and look for rust in the inner valance adjacent to the insides of the front wings.

The Spridget has typical BMC front suspension, though discs are a usefully modern feature. Rack-and-pinion steering is a plus point too. We'll be stripping the suspension in a future episode.

A finger (or pencil) run round wire wheels will reveal the presence of badly loose or broken spokes.

The 1275cc power unit of our car appears fairly healthy with a good oil pressure, but we will be undertaking a full overhaul anyway. Engine bay is reasonably original except for electronic ignition, wrongly positioned coil, and electric fuel pump transposed (like many) from driver's wheel arch to passenger side of engine bay.

mated, because even a brief drive can tell you all sorts of things about a car that otherwise can't be spotted – like whether the gearbox is faulty, the back axle is noisy, whether all the instruments work and so on. Even if you intend to overhaul almost anything (as we do), this still gives you a much better idea of the time scale and probable costs involved in the rebuild.

So after an examination of the bodywork and suspension, partly to make sure that the car was safe enough for the road, off we went with Graham for a round-the-block assessment of the Midget's mechanical state. This revealed that the gearbox was reasonably quiet

with good synchromesh, the diff. was silent, the steering appeared OK, the speedo and rev counter worked but the fuel and water temperature gauges didn't, that the brakes pulled to one side and the clutch was possibly

On road-test, our Midget certainly felt a little worse for wear though not totally 'clapped'.

Driving the car showed up what instruments were faulty; dash layout is reasonably original though apart from a couple of extra switches.

Spridget Rebuild

Off to start a new existence! Our Midget is loaded onto the trailer behind Lindsay Porter's MGB ready for its journey to the workshop and a very great deal of work . . . .

Interior of our Midget needs considerable work, as they say; door trims and part of the facia has been covered with nylon cloth, but who knows, underneath the original material may be in good condition. Steering wheel is non-original.

Dampers were decidedly tired, as a 'bouncing test' at the side of the road quickly showed up.

Hood was presentable, but may look shabby when the car is eventually painted — we'll have to see! Spridgebits partners Graham Sykes and Jed Watts take a look.

suspect. The engine was off-tune rather than worn out, but this is scheduled for a complete strip-down anyway.

The condition of the bodywork and interior is obvious from the pictures, and the true state of the former will be seen more clearly as we come to remove the outer panels. Fortunately there is an increasing range of new panels for the Spridget range, and due to the comparatively large production run of the cars, second-hand trim parts can usually be found where new ones can't. In short, Spridgebits anticipate few problems with replacements and spares for our car, which is a comforting thought for anyone about to embark on the sort of task we have set ourselves.

The work should take about 12 months, and we have a shrewd idea that this Project Car rebuild is going to be fun – and there's always that tempting image of a gleaming Midget dashing through country lanes in summer sunshine to spur us on!

NEXT MONTH
We start the bodywork repairs
and remove the engine
and gearbox.

Spridget Rebuild/2

Paul Skilleter surveys the scene as our Spridget project gets truly under way.

Last month's instalment showed in quite grisly detail the state of our Spridget's body, but before getting to grips with the metalwork, the power unit and exterior trim had to come away. Stripping a car is, of course, the easiest part of a rebuild, and impressive results can be obtained in a very short time; but as the more experienced amongst you will know, the hard bit starts afterwards…

Our car was supplied by Spridgebits of Stoney Lane, Tardebigge near Bromsgrove in Worcestershire (not far off the M5), and they are ideally suited to supply the vast majority of components which we'll need to complete this Project Car. As for the work itself, we're giving the faithful Terry a break (actually he's far too busy with our Swallow and VW Cabriolet rebuilds to take on anything more for a while) and the rebuild is being carried out by Lindsay Porter's Classic Restoration Centre also in Worcestershire. Lindsay, a regular *Practical Classics* con-

Continued

Our 1969 Midget loses its engine, gearbox and exterior trim as the rebuild commences. Paul Skilleter reports.

Spridget Rebuild

First job when removing the engine is to get the bonnet out of the way — it bolts on as shown. Hinge position can be scribed for correct replacement if required.

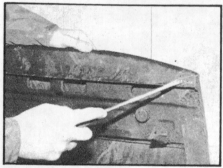

Away from the car, it was now easy to determine the amount of rot in the bonnet's leading edge, a known danger area. You can get a repair section to avoid buying a new bonnet, though with ours we may get away with local patching as it's not too bad.

tributor, originally set up this workshop to provide illustrations for his restoration books, but he now takes on outside work too, and we were pleased to take advantage of this. The fact that it's small (not much bigger than the average double garage) and does not possess exotic equipment means that the approach taken to the rebuild will not differ very much from yours in your own garage at home — a point worth emphasising.

One very grubby radiator is lifted out, after the four bolts holding its shroud to the front panel have been removed. If hoses are being renewed they can be hacksawed to save time.

Next, all the usual disconnections are made — fuel and electrical lines, throttle and choke cables, exhaust, heater pipes etc. Note 'mobile' hoist, useful in confined spaces when car can't be moved.

The procedure for removing the engine differs slightly according to whether you want to take the gearbox out at the same time, as we did, or just the engine. If the latter, the starter needs to be removed first as it bolts through gearbox bellhousing and mounting plate. In any case you need to make all the usual disconnections between engine and car, including the exhaust downpipe — you get at the clamp for this by removing the air filters (carbs can stay on, incidentally). Front engine mountings are dealt with as shown in the pictures, while the rear mounting blocks unbolt from inside the car (two bolts) and underneath (another two bolts).

The Spridget is not a car that is keen to let its engine go, and removing it calls for a bit of juggling on the hoist. Having made all the disconnections, and assuming the box is coming out too, you need to take the weight of the assembly on the crane and then pull forward and shake the unit. This should allow the gearbox to pull free of the propshaft

Engine has to be lifted quite steeply initially to clear steering rack, and for the gearbox remote control to clear the transmission tunnel, where it can get hooked. A bar helps to depress the rear of the engine.

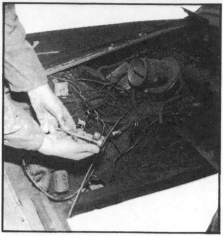

Don't forget to disconnect speedo drive from gearbox before trying to lift, if you are removing gearbox too.

Best technique for removing the engine (it helps greatly on replacement too) is to completely unbolt nearside mounting tower from the chassis, to which it's fixed by four bolts.

On the other side, just the rubber block is unbolted; at the rear, the mounting blocks in their cradle are secured by a total of four bolts.

UJ splines (this rather notorious UJ is enclosed by the tunnel, and re-making this connection has driven owners almost to distraction over the years; a subject we'll therefore be returning to!). This same shaking action should get you free of the rear mounting cradle.

Your next task is to get the fan and sump up and over the steering rack, and the remote control on top of the gearbox clear of the tunnel — the way the engine hangs naturally, this won't occur unless you depress the rear

Next stage was to remove bumpers and such breakables such as lights: rear units are held on by nuts easily accessible from within the boot. Wires on car are colour coded and being plastic, wipe clean, so no tagging should be necessary. Note rotten state of the rear wing after an investigatory paint-strip!

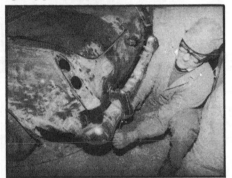

Rear bumper is detached by undoing two bolts per bracket.

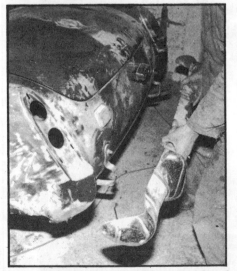

These brackets can be seen clearly in this shot of the bumper being lifted away

Headlight unit and bowl coming away — the latter is almost invariably rusted out and needs replacement.

Front sidelight is removed by taking off plastic lens; lamp body can then be unscrewed from wing. The same applies for the front wiring as for the rear.

Front bumper is simply held on by two nuts which unscrew from fixed bolts projecting from chassis rails (here, nuts have been replaced to avoid loss). Corrosion often presents difficulties though, but these mountings are ideally placed for the application of heat to break any rust bond between nut and bolt.

Whilst in this area, it was decided to remove the air intake trim. Aluminium butting against steel means that, inevitably, the steel securing screws corrode and require drilling out.

Intake trim comes in three sections, one of the two side pieces being shown here.

Spridget Rebuild

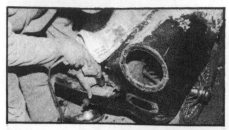

The single lower trim needed drilling out too.

Seats could also be dispensed with at this stage; they are each secured by four bolts into four captive nuts in the floorpan.

of the engine, which thus has to assume a very steep angle as it comes out. An assistant might be quite useful at this stage.

With the power train free of the car, it can be pulled away and carefully lowered to the floor. If you're hiring a crane, you could try getting one with castors as it makes moving the engine around much easier, especially if lack of room prohibits you moving the car itself. But take care, as an engine allowed to swing too violently on the end of a chain could conceivably upset the crane — and remember the old mechanic's adage: never try and stop an engine that is on its way down! It may sound silly, but the natural reaction is often to try to stop it happening, but it's far better to suffer a cracked sump than a broken leg, or worse . . .

Our engine has now been taken away for its strip and rebuild, work which will be covered in detail later on. And to make things a little more interesting, we've decided to incorporate various BMC Special Tuning-type modifications to it, which don't cost a great deal or spoil tractability, but do add to the enjoymnt of the Spridget by providing some extra 'zip'. More of this in a future instalment.

The next immediate step is the big job of getting the bodywork right, however, and to this end the lights and bumpers were taken off. So were the seats, and these can represent something of a tussle because the four bolts holding them in place go into four captive nuts in the floorpan. Of course the cages rust out, and most owners then replace them with ordinary nuts and bolts, which was what had happened on our car.

It's at this stage in a rebuild that you encounter many 'problem' nuts and bolts; sometimes prior soaking with releasing fluid helps, but very often other methods have to be resorted to. In extreme cases there may be no alternative but to drill or saw through the offending item, but heat is a great help and — providing there is no danger of fire or explosion from nearby trim or petrol — the appli-

cation of such will often do the trick. This doesn't mean you have to possess a gas welding kit, as even something like a Ronson blow-torch will produce enough heat to help break the rust bond. A useful and quite cheap addition to the tool-kit if you haven't already got one.

NEXT MONTH
Spridget doors – removal, stripping and re-skinning.

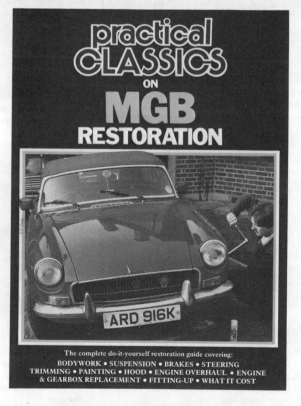

Spridget Rebuild /3

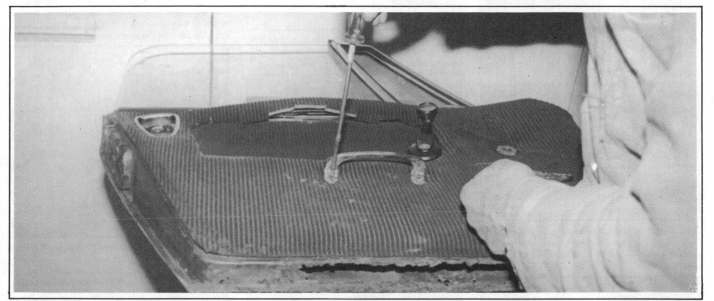

Re-skinning the doors of a Spridget is a job that even a beginner can tackle, and let's face it, most Sprites and Midgets do really need at least one new skin. On our car, the driver's door turned out to be surprisingly good after the paint was stripped, but on the passenger's side it was a different story altogether with a long line of corrosion along the bottom of the skin where it met the frame.

As regular readers will know, we always recommend that a full body rebuild should be centered around the doors and door gaps. It was therefore logical that the first part of the bodywork to be put right should be the doors, which could then be used a bit like templates to check that the correct door-gaps were maintained as the repairs to the hinge pillars, floors and sills — which are next on the list — were undertaken. This was the procedure adopted by Lindsay Porter's Classic Restoration Centre (where our Spridget is

being rebuilt), and the job commenced with the removal of the doors from the car.

This, in fact, is probably the worst part of the re-skinning job as Spridget hinge pillars (including right back to the original Frogeye) are notorious for rusting out. The major damage usually occurs round the bottom hinge mounting, which like the top consists of a captive and theoretically adjustable steel plate attached to the inside of the pillar. The hinge itself is fixed to this plate by means of large Phillips screws. But what happens is that the bottom of the pillar corrodes and so does the metal which is supposed to retain the mounting plate, resulting in a door which is 'loose'.

However, lots of people don't seem to understand the construction of the pillar and so when this occurs they first try welding the hinge directly to the outside of the hinge pillar. That doesn't seem to help so next they weld a strip of metal alongside it. Finally, as Lindsay says, in desperation they start chucking body filler, glass fibre matting,

Gun Gum — anything they can find — into the area of the hinge, hoping that somehow the flapping door will be secured. But of course, the actual hinge mounting is hidden, and in any case the strength has gone out of the pillar because it's rotten at the bottom.

The immediate result of all this is that the bottom hinge is usually very difficult to remove — even if it hasn't been bodged, the screws will probably have seized due to rust. Most likely you will have to drill them out as shown in the pictures; or, especially if you want to limit the work to simply re-skinning the door, you can instead detach the door from the hinges (these are tapped where they meet the door and are secured to the frame by Phillips screws again) and so leave the hinge pillar out of things for the time being.

Anyway, with the door finally on the bench you can strip it of all the 'furniture' (though much of this can be done with the door *in situ* if desired), the first step being to expose the internals by removing the interior handles and trim panels, followed by the

Continued

*Dismantling and re-skinning the doors is the topic this month.
Paul Skilleter continues the story of our 1969 Midget.*

Spridget Rebuild

Door hinges are attached to captive plate inside door pillar by large Phillips screws; ours — like most of them — had to be drilled out at the bottom.

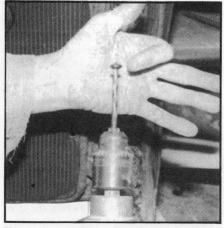

Here you can see how the head of the screw is broken off and trapped as it is drilled; choose a bit which is just smaller than the screw shank diameter.

(continued)

catch mechanism, outer door handle and lock barrel. Next, the window winder mechanism should be unbolted and separated from the glass the latter being lifted up and out of the door after removal of the weatherstrips. The winder mechanism is fiddled free of the door through the holes in the frame lower down.

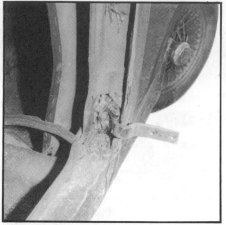

Lower hinge on offside of car was detached from door instead, as the pillar has almost totally disintegrated at the bottom.

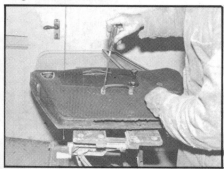

Door furniture removal began with the various handles — all are secured by screws. This shot also shows the extensive rot in the bottom of the door frame.

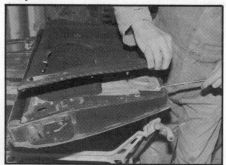

Trim panel (covered with non-original nylon cloth on our car) can then be removed by locating and levering up clips from door frame with screwdriver. If trim backing is badly gone and needs replacement anyway, it may be easier simply to pull the panel away leaving the clips in the door for removal afterwards.

Removal of the quarter-light assembly is a bit of a fiddle: it is held by two bolts at the front edge of the door near the top, and by two more long, hexagonal nuts under the quarterlight itself. Then there's a (7/16 ins) bolt at the bottom of channel extension in which the door glass slides, incorporating a bracket. With all these undone, the assembly can be tilted and wriggled about until it can

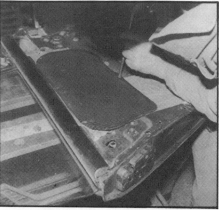

One separate trim panel will remain, and is taken out by undoing self-tapping screws previously hidden by the main panel.

Catch mechanism is released by undoing Phillips screws; on this particular model there are no linkages to worry about, though on later cars the interior handle is remote from the catch and various rods have to be unclipped.

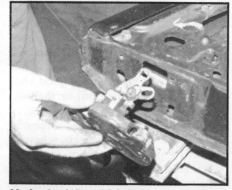

Mechanism being withdrawn from the door.

Exterior door handle is removed by undoing nuts which are are just accessible from inside door frame.

14

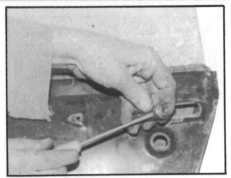

Door lock barrel is secured by a spring clip which is slid out from the inside of the door skin using a screwdriver.

be withdrawn upwards and out of the door. A job which takes longer to do than to write down!

Virtually all the parts for our Spridget are coming from the well-established specialists in this field, Spridgebits, who operate from two addresses — a Birmingham mail-order one, and a 'caller's' one at Tardebigge, not far from Bromsgrove and the M5. The latter also has a large stock of second-hand spares, useful when a new part is not to be found or is too expensive! Needless to say, Spridgebits have a comprehensive and still-growing range of Spridget panels and repair sections, so an off-the-shelf door skin for our own car was easily obtained. Sorry about the wrong phone numbers given in last month's Spridgebits advert by the way – they're correct this time!

Fitting the new skin is relatively easy, though you may well have to repair the door

Old skin is released by grinding away the edges where it is folded over the door frame.

Skin is then split from door using a chisel — not much force should be needed as the metal where it folds over should now be either very thin or non-existent.

On top of the door, the skin is actually spot-welded, and is released by drilling the spot welds on this horizontal face.

The chisel may still be required to separate the skin at this point.

The skin can now be lifted from the door frame, though watch out as thanks to the grinder, some of the edges will be razor sharp. The remains of the lipped-over flanges will mostly fall away from the other side of the frame.

First job before attempting to re-skin was the repair of the door frame; here the entire bottom has been cut away.

The new replacement section was not difficult to fabricate, being a 'T' shape in cross-section with turned-up ends to meet the door frame ends. For more extensively damaged doors, Spridgebits supply a ready-made lower door frame repair section, likewise including the turned-up ends.

Here the new section has been welded into place; continuous welding is unnecessary but brazing afterwards to obtain a water-tight and therefore rot-resistant join is advisable.

The welds being linished smooth on completion; note that the repair panel has not yet been trimmed at the ends.

All traces of rust were ground away from the flanges, which were then dressed flat. The last job before fitting the new skin was to give everything a good coat of zinc-based primer.

The new door skin from Spridgebits, about to be tried on our rebuilt frame.

Spridget Rebuild

The skin comes with flanges bent at right-angles ready for folding over the door-frame edges. When offering up the skin, the holes being pointed out at top must align with those on the door frame; eventually these top faces will be welded.

Here the skin flanges are gradually being folded-over the frame and hammered down — having first checked that the door hasn't distorted during the repair processes. This completes the re-skinning job.

clean-up the door frame properly after you've removed the old skin, as you don't want to trap rust as you fold the new skin over the frame.

One check worth carrying out before you finally tap down the skin or do any welding is to offer up the door with its new skin to the car, to make the door hasn't distorted during the repair operations. Providing your door apertures are correct, this, if it has occured, will show up. Any distortion can quite easily be corrected at this stage simply by twisting the door into shape, the skin only being loosely attached. On obtaining the correct shape, hold it there with a few tack welds along the folds of the skin.

Having made this check, the door skin lips can be tapped down over the frame, using a suitable piece of metal to avoid damaging the door itself where applicable. When this is done, it isn't necessary to weld the skin on all the way round, just two or three tacks on each side being quite sufficient. The only area which really needs welding is on top where the horizontal edges overlap. Your door is then ready for putting back on the car, though this brings the dreaded hinge pillar into the picture again — which is exactly the subject we'll be covering in the January issue.

frame first as we did — it often rots out along the bottom, and if there's a line of rust bubbles in the paintwork of your door at this point, there's a fair chance that both this and the skin itself will need replacing, or at least will require localised repairs. Don't forget to

---

NEXT MONTH
Hinge pillar and sill repair and replacement.

Spridget Rebuild /4

One good thing about restoring a Sprite or a Midget is the range of body panels and repair sections which are becoming available, thanks to the increasing numbers of these cars which are being treated seriously by their owners and so are being properly rebuilt rather than just bodged for the next MoT. Specialists like Spridgebits (of Birmingham and Tardebigge, near Bromsgrove) are responding to the ensuing demand for parts by commissioning items which have long since disappeared from BL's own lists, and by 'inventing' a range of new repair panels especially designed to counter some of the Spridget's better-known rot spots.

As you can see from the pictures, it looks if our own car is going to need a lot of them. But before proceeding with any jobs which might entail a fire risk, Lindsay Porter's Classic Restoration Centre in Worcestershire (where the shell is being rebuilt) removed the petrol tank – a relatively simple job although the studs retaining it do sometimes shear off thanks to rusted nuts, which means the remains have to be drilled out. These can be replaced by ordinary bolts through the boot floor. You could, before returning the tank, braze the heads of new bolts to make re-fitting a one-sided job although the correct studs have very shallow heads and are better.

We'll mention it again when we cover reassembly, but if you are dropping the tank don't forget to refit the wires to the petrol gauge sender *before* you bolt the tank back, because the top of the tank is boxed-in by the boot floor and you can't then get to the sender.

The sills of this car are of vital importance

Our Midget with just some of the repair panels available from Spridgebits – top row, footwell side panel, hinge pillar and skins, door skin, rear wing half; bottom door skin repair section, rear wing lower front repair section, end rear wing repair section, below: inner & outer sills, and rear wheel arch repair section.

to the structure. Removing the outer sill is one of the easiest jobs you'll encounter during the body rebuild of a Spridget, because rust will probably have done most of the work for you. Remove only one sill at a time or the shell will warp. The chisel will be required across the the door aperture however (avoid damaging the inner sill flange at this point just in case you are able to retain the inner sill), and across the bottom of the hinge pillar outer skin if this hasn't already decayed. The lower part of the front wing should be cut away with reference to the intended repair panel to avoid cutting too

much; the opening made here will allow you to separate the outer sill shoulder from the footwell side wall and inner sill – though again, rot will probably have left little for you to do. You should now be able to pull the sill down and cut it away from the bottom of the inner sill. Unless you'e very fortunate, if the outer sill is bad, the inner will almost invariably need replacing too; unfortunately though the bodge of simply fibre-glassing the inner and bunging on a new outer is all too common – but don't be tempted. The shell should be firmly supported to prevent warping. Keep checking the door gap to make sure it isn't shrinking.

At this stage it would be a good idea to consider the construction of the Spridget's bodyshell; a lot of its strength comes from the scuttle/bulkhead assembly and the bulkhead which runs across the car behind the seats (and contains the rear spring anchorages of

Continued

Sills, wings and hinge pillars feature this month as we get to grips with our '69 Midget's bodyshell. Paul Skilleter brings you the latest.

Spridget Rebuild

Petrol tank is secured by studs projecting from boot floor, but sometimes these shear as the nuts are undone necessitating drilling the studs out from floor as shown.

Don't disconnect fuel filler until you've completed any drilling, as it will prevent sparks from igniting fuel vapour. Obviously, never use heat on those studs!

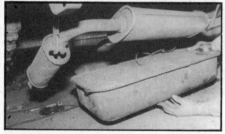

With all nuts undone, tank can be dropped from under car after fuel pipe has been disconnected. Wiring to petrol gauge is only accessible after tank is dropped (not to be forgotten when replacing same…).

which we'll have much to say in the future). But a good proportion of the 'length-wise' strength is also contributed by the inner and outer sills which together form a box section running virtually from front wheel to rear wheel, plus the footwell side panel, the hinge pillar, and the door shut panel and rear wing side.

The danger is that if the car is simply left on its wheels, it will sag in the middle. This means that if you welded the new panels in without further ado, you could end up with a banana-shaped Spridget…After some experimentation, we found the best way of supporting the car was to jack all four wheels off the ground and place axle stands directly under the suspension; then to avoid the shell sagging in the middle, it was supported under the transmission tunnel at the point

All the signs of extensive decay in front wing and sill; reasonable appearance of hinge pillar skin means nothing – it's easily fudged and the vital pillar behind which carries the door is usually in a poor way.

where cross-member runs across the car on top of the floor on each side of the tunnel (in line with the jacking points). You are helped here by the fact that the Spridget floor is a flat panel enclosing almost all the length of the tunnel. Then by lifting or dropping this central support, it was quite easy to get the shell dead true – and it left plenty of room to work on the sill areas.

As we said in previous episodes, on nearly all cars which are undergoing advanced structural repairs the thing to do is 'build around the door gaps', and this is why our first bodywork job on the Spridget was to reskin the doors (and afterwards offer them up to the car to ensure they hadn't distorted); that job was covered in the last (December) issue. These rebuilt doors now become templates to check the door apertures as the shell is being repaired.

You will have noted from the picture sequence that the lower part of the rear wing was cut away at the same time as the sill, using the 'half-wing' repair panel as a template – ensure that

Outer sill is cut through just outboard of where its flange meets the inner sill in the door gap.

Cut is continued under hinge pillar skin; lower part of front wing is cut away within the area of the relevant repair section (if you are not going to replace the whole wing).

this is offered-up correctly before scribing your line. As the edges of this are rebated to obtain a flush fit, your actual cut line will be ½ inch below the scribed line to allow for the overlap. This panel is also shown in the heading picture, along with a simpler one just covering the wheel-arch, and another which replaces the lower rear section of the wing below the lights – you take your choice according to how badly the original wing is damaged. If the top section of the wing is also rusty, a whole new wing will be required.

After chiselling through where front of sill meets the footwell side panel, sill will usually fold down to reveal all…

It didn't need much to detach the outer sill from the bottom part of the equally rotten inner. Watch those chiselled edges – they'll be very sharp.

With the car sliced open in this way, it was possible to obtain a very accurate picture of the work needed to repair the internal structure of the car – that is, the front footwell side, hinge pillar, inner sill, rear wheel arch and the box sections behind the rear wheel. You can only guess so much from looking at outer panels. We judged our car to be in pretty poor shape, but very typical of a sports car subjected to some fourteen British winters without any protection from the salt spray which is part of them. It could have been worse – but not much..!

The next task was to repair or replace the

Rear wing is dealt with next – paint stripper had previously revealed holes in arch and in rear section.

The Spridgebits repair panel is held up to wing, carefully positioned and a line scribed.

The old section is cut away along a line drawn ½ inch under the original one, as new panel will be overlapped. The cut is made down edge of rear light panel and then follows the rear seam.

At the front, the metal is cut ½ inch back from shut pillar; wing had rotted through at bottom so didn't require any tools to separate it there.

hinge pillars so that the doors could be remounted. On the nearside of the car it was decided to replace just the bottom two-thirds of the hinge pillar – there's a lot to be said for leaving parts in if perfectly sound, even if it makes the job take slightly longer, as the original item helps you correctly locate the other part. Sometimes, of course, the part is so badly damaged that you have no option but to replace it, and this was the case with the hinge pillar on the offside of the car (which will be shown next month). The nearside one wasn't so bad, and so the Spridgebits pillar was cut to match the damaged portion removed; aligning the new section correctly

With wing removed, the usual extensive rot was visible in the inner sill structure. Note that our re-skinned door has already been replaced to keep tabs on the door gap.

Rear box sections were equally corroded (the Frogeye is of simpler construction here, having only one box section); and just look at that inner wing!

was made easy by projecting a straight-edge down from the original top, while at the bottom, the remains of the old inner sill showed the position too.

Even then, at this stage the pillar was only spot-brazed into place to allow for any later small adjustments which might be necessary to obtain a perfect door fit – the braze could simply be softened by the torch until plastic, and the pillar moved to suit. Some restorers would advocate using self-tapping screws to allow adjustment to be made – with no distortion of the scuttle inner panel – and screws also hold the pillar in 'flush'.

After supporting car correctly (a vital point – see text) thought can be given to removing metal. This is the footwell side repair panel, shown before the body was cut into.

Spridget Rebuild

Particularly if hinge pillar alone is to be replaced (without necessarily the entire inner sill structure), it's the footwell side which must also be made good as the new pillar will be welded to it. Here the panel is being tied-up.

The area it must replace is shown in this picture of the footwell side panel, in which plenty of holes can be seen up to eight inches above the equally rotten inner sill.

Front wing should be removed by unbolting from front valance (these two bolts are probably the worst and may need heat), front panel (another two), and at rear.

It is just possible to fit a new hinge pillar skin by undoing the rear bolts only, as the new skin will be held in place by the three vertical bolts which secure the wing at the rear, but this isn't recommended as you haven't the space to repair or weld the area properly.

This shot, taken at a later stage with the new inner sill fitted, shows how much more access you have to the pillar structure and footwell side panel with the wing removed completely. Lindsay is holding the tattered remnants of the original inner sill.

The hinge pillar is also located by the footwell side panel, which can be repaired at about the same time. On our Spridget a repair panel was used which replaced the bottom half of the side panel, though Frogeye owners might like to note that they might be advised to replace the whole side panel on their cars as this area shows when the Frog bonnet (complete with 'wings') is lifted, as a seam would not look original. The repair panel we used was a little less satisfactory

On the nearside, only the bottom half of the new Spridgebits pillar was required – the discarded top part, incorporating the captive hinge plate, is shown alongside.

Hinge pillar skin: the original skin was previously cut away (using grinder on the edges as per door skin removal) using the replacement section to mark the point at which the scuttle must be cut. Wing and door are in place to check positioning of new pillar skin.

than others as it didn't quite cover the full length of the footwell – it should run from toe-board, then behind the pillar, to the door aperture, but was a little short and had to have a strip added. That aside, it did the job well, and the installation of this and other panels will be covered in the next issue.   □

NEXT MONTH
Fitting inner and outer sills complete hinge pillar assembly, and cutting out the floors.

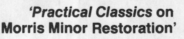

Spridget Rebuild /5

L ast month we promised to follow the procedure involved in replacing a hinge pillar assembly complete, as opposed to just the bottom half as was shown in the last episode. But before we begin, can we stress the importance of avoiding distortion of the shell during the replacement of structural members like these, and remind you of the precautions Lindsay Porter's Classic Restoration Centre is taking in this respect.

During all these operations, therefore, the car is being supported on all four corners under the suspension, and under the transmission tunnel where the above-floor crossmember joins it. By lifting or dropping this centre support it is possible to influence the width of the door gap, which is checked both by measuring from one side to the other, and by re-hanging the rebuilt doors. A check should also be kept that the car is not 'lozenging', though this is unlikely if major components like sills and pillars are removed from only one side of the car at a time.

Returning to the subject of hinge pillars, the outer skin is scribed at the top after offering up the new pillar skin and then cut away as shown in the pictures. The hinge pillar itself, which of course carries all the weight of the door, is then removed from the scuttle side by drilling the spot-welds carefully (usually you can get away without going right through, just weakening enough for them to break on being levered). The new pillar was then installed and tacked lightly in place, and the re-skinned door replaced to check that all was well. In this instance the outer skin had already been fitted to the pillar off the car, unlike the other side where only part of the pillar was replaced and the complete skin added afterwards.

The car now had both hinge pillars replaced, so that both doors could be re-hung

at will to check the door gaps as work proceeded on other parts of the car. The next major component to be replaced was the nearside inner sill, basically a long, flat length of steel and like all the other components we've used, readily obtainable from Spridgebits, the well-known Sprite and

Midget specialists. They, as you probably know by now, hail from the Birmingham district but mail-order countrywide. Note that the inner sills must be installed with the flange at their front edges turned outwards, so don't muddle-up an offside with a nearside one for this reason.

Hinge pillar skin was removed by cutting at scuttle, and by using grinder on vertical edges.

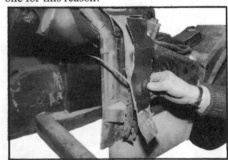

This leaves a lot of sharp edges so watch out! Hinge pillar itself is then revealed.

Continued

Fitting new sills and hinge pillars are among the topics this time. Paul Skilleter continues the Spridget story.

Spridget Rebuild

Spot-welds holding old pillar to scuttle are drilled and broken, and the pillar removed.

This is the Spridget's new pillar, the inside face containing the cages for the plates into which the door hinges mount.

The original inner sill was easily separated from the car — hardly anything was holding it at the bottom where it met the floor, so there just remained some spot-welds to break at the door pillars and some at the rear structure. Next, wherever the new inner sill would meet the bodywork, the area had to be trimmed and/or cleaned-up to accept it, particularly the square-section cross-member flanges which needed dressing with hammer and dolly, and the area immediately behind the door shut pillar.

The sill also meets the footwell side-wall, running along outboard of it, in fact, with the

On this side of car, new hinge pillar and skin are pre-assembled and fitted to car as a unit — a simple matter of laying the pillar on the skin and tapping the flanges over.

The assembly can then be fitted to car, using wing mounting bolt holes to help align the pillar. Note below that the new bottom section of footwell wall has been fitted too.

wall overlapping the sill in a downwards direction on the inside of the car. The replacement section of 'wall' had been fitted just previously, the original wall having been cut off about half-way down to match the repair section, which was then welded to it in an overlapping join. As for the floor, this was due for replacement so it just remained to tidy it back enough for it not to interfere with the new sill; if in the rather unlikely event the floor was in good condition along its outer edges and was to be retained, then it too would have to be dressed flat to meet the sill neatly.

This done, the new sill was clamped up to the body and carefully aligned. This procedure is followed in the photographs but it is worth emphasising how important it is to get the height of the sill correct in relation to the door gap, and to arrive at the right gap between sill and the door itself. Use the opposite side of the car as a guide (one reason for doing just a side at a time!) if you aren't sure of how these dimensions should look. When you think you've got everything right, you can tack the inner sill in place, and after yet

Returning to the nearside, here the new inner sill is about to be tried up; car is supported at all four suspension points and in the centre to maintain its 'trueness'.

Inner sill in place, with door in shut position to check clearances and alignment (particularly height) of sill. Cross-member flanges (right) should be dressed flat on removing old inner sill.

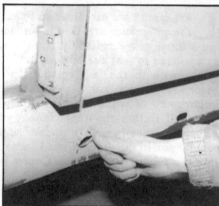

The jacking point which protrudes from this same cross-member on the outside is one of many reference points for the correct placing of the inner sill; obviously though, if the jacking point needs replacement or repair this needs to be done before the new inner sill is finally fitted.

Front end of sill lines up with inner wing flange as it sweeps down — or the remains of it! Sill is secured to new footwell side with tack-welds when correctly positioned .

further checks, including with both door and outer sill offered up, you can weld securely at shut pillars, cross-member flanges and footwell wall.

Inner and outer sills can, in fact, be assembled together off the car and installed as a unit, though on the nearside of the Spridget they were put on separately. So next the outer sill was clamped up and after the usual checks (you can't do enough of these!) spot-welded to the inner sill and gas-welded to the car structure.

At the rear, sill abutts rear inner wing flange, though on our car this has virtually disappeared. Tack-welds secure it to inner structure behind door-shut pillar.

When the inner sill is fitting correctly, the outer one can be offered up. Hinge pillar skin is not yet on. Note that outer sill flange slots up in gap between bottom of hinge pillar and footwell side.

A trolley jack is handy in positioning outer sill — door has been taken off in order to weld inner and outer sill together, after clearances had once again been checked. Note central support for car under transmission tunnel/cross-member.

Spot-welding the flanges of inner and outer sills together. Plug or tack welding with gas or arc produces the same result but takes a lot longer and is much less neat.

Hinge pillar skin is positioned (it had previously been trial-fitted to sort out join with scuttle at top) and spot-welded to footwell 'wall'. It is also tacked lightly to outer sill at bottom.

The car is now strong enough for the floor to be removed — simply a case of chiselling inboard of the transmission tunnel, front cross-member and rear bulkhead flanges.

Here the very rusty floor drops away. Next step will be to remove remains of floor from perimeter flanges and clean up the latter ready for the new floor — but that comes a little later.

At this stage, with the car stiffened very considerably thanks to the new sills, it was decided to remove the nearside floor. This was done in two sections, the footwell and seat areas, these being chiselled free inboard of the flanges to which they had originally been spot-welded. The remaining bits of floor still attached to the transmission tunnel and cross-member were removed afterwards, by drilling and 'worrying' the spot-welds free. The flanges were then dressed ready for accepting a new floor section, the installation of which will be covered in a later episode.

As can be seen, a lot of repairs are now required from the door shut pillar back, beginning with the shut face itself which had rotted at the bottom. A little repair section

Shut pillar needed repair at bottom, and here the affected part has been cut away and the pillar cleaned-up.

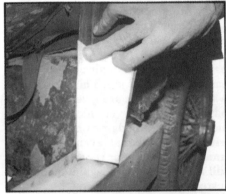

A cardboard template is made, covering the area to be replaced.

The new section, a relatively simple one, is made up on the bench, using vice and panel-beating hammer. Here a crease is being put into it to obtain a flush fitting (see text).

This entails 'rebating' the top flange which goes behind the shut pillar, and the outer flange which will meet the new outer wing when that is fitted

CONTINUED ON PAGE 68

Spridget Rebuild /6

It's the sometimes tedious work of repairing a car's inner structure that takes up most of the time spent rebuilding a bodyshell, fitting the major outer panels often (but not always) being the easiest part of the job. This is of course why so many cars are given new outer panels which look very nice, but suffer any amount of bodging underneath — with the result that eventually, continuing rust and poor repairs take their toll and the car once again becomes a festering, dangerous heap.

Needless to say, *Practical Classics* project cars aren't treated that way and Lindsay Porter's Classic Restoration Centre take a similar view, hence the many painstaking hours that are being spent on the Midget's shell. The major repair covered this month is that to the car's inner rear wheel arches, which as our heading picture shows were seen to be in a pretty poor state on removal of the outer wings.

There are at least two ways to do this job, and both of them are shown in detail; you can make your own repair sections, or you can buy the excellent repair panel supplied by companies such as Spridgebits. As the pic-

ture sequences clearly demonstrate, it is far quicker – and neater come to that – to use the latter.

A couple of additional points can be stressed here; if you are using the 'piecemeal' method (possibly more applicable if only part of the arch is rust damaged), make sure you only tack the made-up sections to the wheel arch very lightly at first, so that altering their positions is easy — modifications of this sort may well be necessary when you try up the outer panel (as you should do at every oppor-

tunity) and find that the flanges aren't meeting, or that the repair sections are preventing the outer wing from seating properly. Bear in mind (if you haven't done a similar job before) that the inner wheel arch mirrors the contour of the outer wing at this point, which means that fairly accurate work with hammer and dolly is necessary to obtain a 'clean' fit between the two. A similar checking procedure must be carried out when fitting the complete Spridgebits panel too.

To the rear of the wheelarch, and also

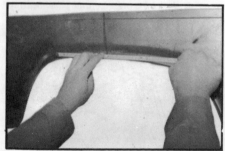

'Knife and fork' method of repairing the damaged inner rear wing seen in our heading picture begins with marking off new outer wing in four sections to act as curvature templates for the four inner wing repair sections.

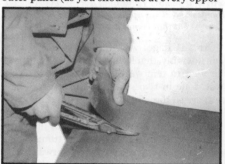

First repair section to be made will cover the area adjacent to the door shut pillar, and a suitable length of 22 gauge steel sheet is cut.

Using hammer and dolly, the piece of sheet is, after trimming to correct curvature, shaped accordingly.

Continued

Two methods of repairing inner rear wings this month, plus fitting an outer rear wing repair section. Paul Skilleter and Lindsay Porter report.

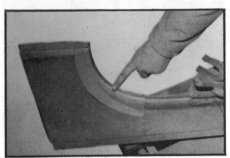

The new outer wing section is used from time to time in order to check whether the correct shape is being produced — the two of course must eventually meet.

Here the first repair section has been offered up and both it and the existing inner wing trimmed to match. It is then tacked lightly into place.

Close-up of the end of the repair section, showing where the next piece will join . . .

. . . while as a check on its position, the outer wing is tried up — the pencil indicates again where the inner wing repairs come up to at this stage.

Now the second section is made, using a piece of angle iron clamped to the bench while obtaining the initial rough 'tuck under' required.

Hammer and dolly are once again used to create the proper curvature, and the flange which will eventually meet the outer wing.

The relevent length of inner wing has been trimmed, and here the second repair section is being MIG-welded into place at intervals.

enclosed by the outer wing, are box sections which are in effect extensions of the boot floor. These usually rust out, and new ones were made accordingly. The shell here is clearly based on the original Frogeye's, and to compensate for the extra width at this point (Frogs had different rear wings that swept in at the back), BMC just added on another bit of metal which was spot-welded to what had been the original fillet between boot and wing. Frog-eyes are thus simpler to

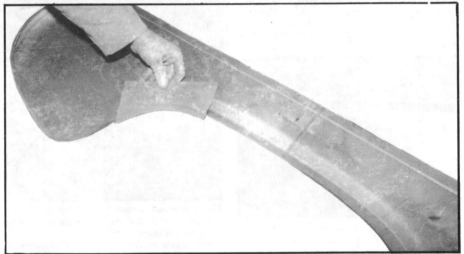

For the next section, a cardboard pattern was made, again taken from the outer wing.

After more work at the bench, the third new piece of inner wheel arch is ready.

A device like this (found in decorators' shops amongst other places!) is useful in checking contours — it can be set against the outer wing and then offered up to the repair piece.

Spridget Rebuild

This is welded into place, and this picture shows the last section in position too. Also, the two (triangular) boot floor extensions have been made up and fitted.

repair at this point, as indeed are their rear wheelarches, a job which will be covered next month — we are, in fact, including a number of bodywork jobs peculiar to the Frog in this series, to make it relevent to owners of these cars too.

Work has progressed more quickly than these reports and our Project Car Spridget's bodyshell is complete as you read this, with the suspension currently being rebuilt and refitted. In fact, within a couple of issues we should be able to show you pictures of the completed car – just in time for the spring!

The new section has been spot-welded into place, and here the welds are being linished flat. If you haven't a spot-welder, use plug welds with your gas or arc welder — a continuous weld could produce distortion in such large unsupported areas of metal.

Here the new outer section has been made up and fitted to these extension pieces. After further trial fitting of the outer wing, the wheel arch repair sections are finally welded continuously to the wheel arch.

New outer panel is also welded to inner wing flanges around wheel arch circumference; preferably, this area should be flooded with braze afterwards to prevent ingress of water. Meanwhile the waistline join is being lead-loaded to complete the repair.

In contrast to the previous method, fitting the Spridgebits inner wing panel is a 'piece of cake' according to Lindsay. First it is offered up to the car and a line scribed.

The new panel is then butt-welded to the car, making a very easy and neat repair. The new outer wing should be tried up first however, to make sure the inner wing is correctly positioned.

This view shows how the outer repair panel joins at the rear, its flanges lipped over the remaining part of the original outer wing's lamp panel. Similar flanges lip over the door shut panel at the front end, and are also spot or plug welded.

The area thus defined is cut away; this of course is being shown on the opposite side of the car, where the rear wing, which will be replaced entirely, has been roughly cut away to allow access.

Meanwhile, on the other side, inner wheelarch repairs are complete and the outer wing repair section can be positioned. The rebated edge allows a flush fit along the waistline, where the metal was previously marked and then cut away after offering up the new panel carefully.

NEXT MONTH
Fitting a complete rear wing, more about sills, and Frog-eye rear-end repairs.

Spridget Rebuild /7

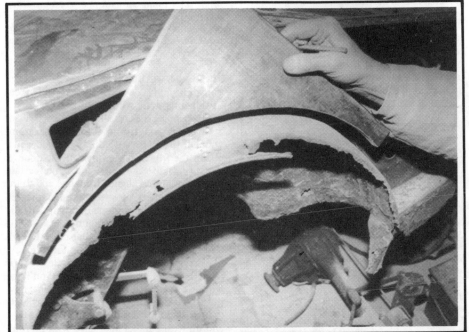

Frog-eyes enter the scene this time round, because as promised, we're also including any jobs which are unique to the earlier car. These include the rear spring mounting repairs (to come later), and the inner rear wings which are covered here.

The early cars have curved instead of square-topped wheel apertures, and Frog-eye rear-end construction in general is a little simpler than later Austin Healey Sprites and Midgets. It's the outer rim of the inner wing which tends to rust, where moisture is trapped between it and the outer rear wing — which of course needs to be removed or cut away so that you can obtain access. Lindsay Porter's Classic Restoration Centre (which operates from near Worcester — tel: Upper Sapey 695) specialises in the repair of Frog-eyes — plus later Spridgets — and the repair of this area is shown in the picture sequences.

Obviously your new repair section must cover the area of rusty inner wing to be removed, but other than that the only critical part of its shape is the flange where it will join the outer wing. When you are making up the section (or sections) involved, then, first tack them very lightly in place and offer up the outer wing or repair section. This will allow you to adjust them so that they meet the outer panel neatly all the way round the wheel aperture. The picture applying to this job shows two Frogs – one is to have a complete new rear wing, the old one being roughly cut away, while the second has had only enough metal removed for the fitting of a repair section. Both these panels (plus a lot more!) are available from Spridgebits who are supplying virtually all the parts used in our Spridget rebuild.

Returning to our 1969 Midget, we show this month the installation of the offside sill — but as an assembly with the inner sill this time, instead of first the inner and then the outer as on the previous side. The work

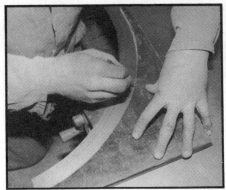

Frog-eye inner rear wing commences with making a simple pattern from plywood, following the shape of the inner wing where it will be cut away. The outline is then transferred onto sheet steel (above), allowing enough width to cover the area on the car to be cut away.

The same bit of ply is used to help produce the flange on the repair section, where it will eventually meet the new outer wing.

Continued

More inner rear wing and sill-fitting techniques this month, plus the installation of a complete new rear wing. Paul Skilleter and Lindsay Porter bring you the latest.

Spridget Rebuild

Here is the finished job (actually on another Frog); it will probably be made up of several sections fitted one after the other. Some curvature will need to be introduced into the new sections, to match that of the existing inner wing.

involved in preparing the shell is much the same however, and we have already covered the replacement of the all-important hinge pillar and its outer skin. Again, you really need to remove the front wing for satisfactory access, and the footwell side wall (or bul-

Spridget sill fittings: as an alternative to the method shown in a previous issue, outer and inner sill can be joined away from the car and fitted as an assembly.

This is where it will go, with new hinge pillar already in place and bulkhead side panel cut back to good metal. Note cross-member under pillar-flange; ends of this must be made good if damaged as they are eventually welded to inner sill.

Sill assembly clamped in place; bottom half of side panel (footwell 'wall') has been replaced. Location points include jacking point hole under pillar (and lining-up with floor cross-member), and front end of sill which continues the curve of the front wheel arch. New jacking point can be fitted during these operations if it's needed, or at a later stage.

khead side) will undoubtedly need its bottom half replacing — a section is available from Spridgebits along with the sills.

Once more, the crucial point is to carry out a thorough trial-fitting before you commit yourself to any final welding. Therefore just clamp the sills in place, then fit the door (if you've had to remove it) and make certain that everything is aligned from one end to the other, and that (most important) the sill *height* is correct across the door gap. Ideally this should be done in conjunction with the fitting of the rear wing so that this, the sills and the door can all be lined up together.

Make sure, of course, that the door is indeed hung properly otherwise you'll be working to an incorrect reference point; having done that, line up sill and rear wing (which includes the door shut face) so you end up with parallel door gaps with no fouling. Some people like to temporarily fit the

Rear end of sill also matches curvature of rear wheel arch (if there's any left!). Here sill assembly is being supported while positioning is checked in relation to door, which must be fitted for this purpose.

After very careful checking (including to see if car is 'square') the sill assembly is spot-welded in place. Gas welding is used where door pillars meet sill.

rubber door seals at this stage to see if they make any difference to the fit.

Jacking points: these are in the form of brackets which sit in the ends of the cross-members which run out from the transmis-

Only late-type complete seal wings are available (we were lucky), which are different under the rear light. They can be altered.

First the old wing must come off; hood rail and associated chrome trim pieces must be removed so you can get at the line of spot welds at top.

The old wing is cut away all round where its flanges meet the car; it is then easy to drill the spot welds which hold the flanges on and — taking care not to damage the matching flange on the shell — remove them bit by bit, using Molegrips or similar to finally break the weakened spot welds (no need to drill right through both pieces of metal).

Having dollied the car flanges straight and ground off any remaining bits of weld or surface rust, the new wing can be offered up for a trial fit.

Again, it's crucial that the door is in place so that alignment with this can be checked. Levels at top and shoulder must be right, and so must the vertical gap.

The old wing was cut away just outboard of centre of lamp panel — but here we have a problem — light apertures don't match! However, as the light units still fit we went ahead.

When the fit is absolutely correct, the wing can be spot-welded to the tonneau panel flanges.

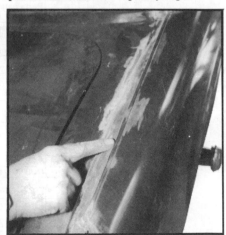

Beading on top comes with new wing. Flanges along here are welded from inside boot. The wing is also gas-welded at beginning of beading adjacent to cockpit, at the rear, and down lamp panel.

Bottom of wing near door is tacked to end of sill, and wing/sill flanges welded together from inside the wheelarch.

The repaired inner wing flanges are welded to the new outer wing round the wheel-arch circumference; here the welds are being finished off.

There was a small area of damage on the rear panel inboard of the new wing which meant a small patch being let-in; this was then lead-loaded.

sion tunnel to end at the inner sills underneath the hinge pillars. You can plan to fit them during the replacement of the sills, or they can actually be replaced separately afterwards. This, together with fitting new cross-member ends, will be covered later. Incidentally, if you have any doubts about the strength of your Spridget in this area, don't use the jacking points at all as they are notoriously prone to breaking off, in which case (quite apart from the danger to life and limb involved) the jack can cause considerable damage to the sills as the car collapses.

We've already covered the fitting of a rear wing repair panel (which comes half-way up the car), and this month we show a complete rear wing being mounted on our Spridget. Genuine BL wings for this model were recently discontinued, though you can alter the late-type wing (which is still listed) under the !amp panel if your wish – but most people get away with repair sections. Lamp panels differed anyway, but frankly, if the light units still fit, this is not a matter for great concern as this area isn't visible on an assembled

Spridget Rebuild

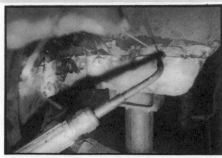

The affected strip of metal was cut away and replaced with a made-up repair section. Spot-welder wouldn't reach in here so the gas torch was used; the join was waterproofed afterwards with braze and seam-sealer.

car, but if you are a purist (or if the lamps don't fit), it is quite an easy matter to release the old lamp panel from your original wing (it almost certainly won't have rusted at this point) and transfer it to the new wing.

Once again, the trial fit is all-important and particular attention should be paid to the front end of the wing where it meets the door

There remained a line of rot at the rear of the inner wing, and all old sealant, paint and rust-scale was cleaned off to show the full extent of the damage.

— as already mentioned, an irregular door gap or door/wing shoulder line will be very noticeable when the car is painted! All the flanges on the car to which the wing will be

welded must be cleaned and straightened first, of course. The Classic Restoration Centre, like most professionals, make extensive use of the spot welder for welding flanges together but this is more for speed than anything else, and you will be able to obtain just as good a job with careful gas or arc welding — which in any case is necessary at certain attachment points where the arms of the spot-welder won't reach. □

NEXT MONTH
Replacing the floors.

Spridget Rebuild /8

Having restored some strength to the car's shell by replacing inner and outer sills plus the hinge pillars, the floor could safely be removed — though Lindsay Porter's Classic Restoration Centre was again very careful to check that the shell was 'all square' with the door gaps correct before doing so.

The fact that the original floor rarely rusts under the transmission tunnel means that this is usually left in place, providing an ideal spot to support the car in addition to the front suspension points, and under the front corners of the (now repaired) boot floor. If the shell has distorted slightly, its shape can be influenced by lowering or raising the front or rear ends of the car, or by doing the same from the centre by altering the height of a trolley jack used under a stout length of timber running under the transmission tunnel. Door gaps are checked by offering up the doors themselves, and by measuring side-to-side. But with the new sills in place and with equalised support as described, you shouldn't run into trouble.

When removing the old floor, leave the spring and its mounting plate in place at this

stage — very little will probably be holding it to the floor and bulkhead anyway, as most cars are in the condition that you can see ours is at this point! This will help you position the new floor correctly and, when you start on repairing the rear bulkhead, will help in the positioning of new parts for this too.

The complete floor we used from Spridgebits was an excellent pressing containing the correct footwell and the strengthening flutes under the seats. After cleaning up the car flanges it slotted into place with a minimum of panel-beating, the only annoying thing being that it didn't quite reach the transmission tunnel, leaving a three-inch gap to fill if you've taken the original floor completely out. When the floor, held in place by Molegrips and axle stands from underneath, had been accurately fitted, it was spot-welded to the seams and gas

welded to the inner sill (if MIG or gas spot plug welding, floor flanges should be drilled beforehand of course). The only part not welded at this stage was where the floor

Floor was removed by cutting inboard of flanges, either side of cross-member which is left in place at this stage; note that new inner and outer sills are in position.

Remains of old floor still attached to flanges on transmission tunnel etc. need to be removed, and flanges dressed straight.

New floors and repairs to the rear bulkhead leave only the front end of the body to do — Paul Skilleter reports on our 1969 Midget complete restoration.

Spridget Rebuild

Trying the new floor up from underneath; its flanges needed slight modification to fit the inner sill neatly (as is being done here) and other parts of the car.

Here is the floor in position; note pressings which add strength — replacing with simple sheet steel is not really good enough. Note that rusted section of cross-member (containing jacking point) has been removed, but corroded rear bulkhead (foreground) where spring mounts has been left for now.

approached the rear bulkhead, where metal still had to be replaced.

Floor fitting is easy compared to repairing the rear bulkhead. Spridgebits, who've been in the business of supplying parts for Sprites and Midgets longer than most, have developed an increasingly useful range of repair panels for this area, but the job is still definitely not an easy one.

Lindsay Porter compares the Spridget's rear bulkhead to a bar of Toblerone – it's a triangular-shaped box section tapering at the top with divisions at intervals to strengthen

Underneath, showing strengthening rail on new floor adjacent to prop. tunnel, which helps support the seats on top. Sound old floor is left on tunnel.

As could be seen on previous picture, new floor doesn't quite reach tunnel, so length of steel has to be cut to fit gap.

New length of cross-member was folded to shape, and an adapted MGB jacking point (with cut-down straps) welded in position.

New section was then cut exactly to length, so it met remaining original cross-member, and butted-up to sill wall correctly on the outside.

Floor (and extension) was then welded into place all round, stopping short of rear bulkhead, and cross-member was welded to floor. Gas and MIG welding was used for this job.

Rear bulkhead repair sections available from Spridgebits include spring mounting plate, the floor surrounding it, and (foreground) vertical section of rear bulkhead behind seats which spring mounting plate bolts up to.

it. Besides stiffening the whole shell, it does the all-important job of carrying the forward mountings of the rear ½-elliptic leaf springs. The end of each spring actually mounts within a detachable, self-contained plate which in turn is bolted up under the bulkhead, the four bolts passing through the floor and through two of those divisions where they are flanged over on top of the floor. The nuts are welded on the plate itself for the two leading bolts, but are welded to the bulkhead division flanges to take the rearmost bolts. To remove a rear spring, the plate must be dropped otherwise you can't get at the shackle pin of course, which is out of sight up inside the bulkhead.

This is a complete rear wall of the bulkhead, which faces the back axle; on our car it was more convenient to use just sections of it – one section (right) has been cut off in readiness.

The offside spring mounting area on our Spridget, showing how this part of the bulkhead had rusted away to almost nothing — the spring and its mounting plate have virtually no support at all. Dangerous collapse could have followed.

Spring and plate were removed (captive nut for latter is visible to left of sill) and so was the damper, though its nuts needed some heat to persuade them! Note rust damage further up bulkhead too.

Spring mounting area of bulkhead was cut back to sound metal and cleaned up with grinder.

With floor supported in correct position by board and stands underneath, the job of building up the various sections of the bulkhead could begin. This internal wall is having its bottom third (which incoporates one of the captive nuts for spring mounting plate) replaced.

Spring mounting plate can now be fitted, as shown by this view from under the car. The Spridgebits floor comes pre-drilled with the holes for this.

The bulkhead on the other (nearside) of the car was possibly even worse; here the painstaking job of building up the compartments with new sections can be seen underway, either side of the triangular damper-mounting plate.

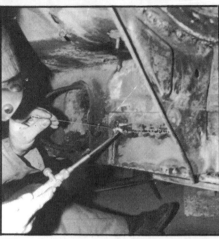

When all the internal 'walls' had been repaired, the bulkhead could be closed-off from the rearwards side using sections taken from the complete panel shown previously.

Repair of the area is a matter of replacing the bottom third or so of the outer bulkhead members. The floor, once correctly positioned tight against the flanges which still do exist, provides a good base to work

Some of the work is done from inside the car too. Here a new section of the internal wall is about to be fitted.

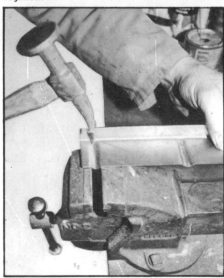

This was made up on the bench, the fluting reproduced as shown.

Continued

The Spridgebits panel which closes off the bulkhead above the spring mounting being offered up.

from, and offering up the new spring mounting plate which ensure you correctly site any new bolt holes. When the internal divisions are repaired, the bulkhead is closed-off from the axle side (a complete panel is available but as it's usually only the outer parts of the bulkhead which corrode, it isn't often necessary to embark on the much more lengthy job of installing it complete). This can be followed by the same job from inside the car, using the easy-to-fit section directly over the spring mounting which is supplied by Spridgebits, and made-up sections taking care of any additional gaps.

As the pictures show, rot extended into the

Here is the same panel being welded up on the other side of the car; it is easily positioned thanks to holes at the bottom through which the spring mounting plate bolts go.

wheel-arch and higher areas of the bulkhead, this damage being countered by cutting out the affected areas and letting-in shaped patches. While you're in this area, check the condition of the damper mounting panel (another triangular piece of metal extending rearwards from the bulkhead) and repair as necessary. Finally, clean everything down to bright metal and paint with rust-resistant primer.

On both sides rust damage extended up into the wheelarch, which required patching as shown here.

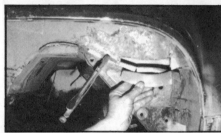

Some of these repairs went back over the damper mounting panel, and affected areas had to be cut out and replaced by patches.

NEXT MONTH
Frogeye Sprite ¼-elliptic spring mounting repairs

Spridget Rebuild/9

When Healeys were asked in 1956 by Leonard Lord, then head at BMC, to design a baby playmate for the 'Big' Healey, the response from the Warwick-based design team was really quite adventurous. The 'Frogeye' Sprite, as it was much later to become known, was the first British sportscar not to have a separate chassis, the front lights were intended to be of the type used nowadays by certain exotic Porsches where the glasses lie exposed and staring to the heavens when the lamps are extinguished and the rear suspension was to be of the quarter-elliptic pattern *a la* Mk I Jaguar which preceded it.

The pop-up headlamps were dropped in favour of the 'frogeyes' which have become

If a 'Frogeye' is so badly corroded that the door gaps open up like this at the bottom-front edge, the sills have certainly corroded very badly. When a car has got to this stage, it's almost certain that the heelboards and perhaps the spring boxes will be affected too, although the spring boxes themselves are made of thicker plate and could outlast the metal surrounding supporting them.

the little car's trademark but the monocoque, chassis-less construction and the quarter-elliptics remained. Ironically, although these developments represented a great step at the time, they are now the very areas that give the owner, buyer and restorer the biggest headaches. Such is progress!

Rusty 'Frogeyes' suffer from the dreaded droops amidships just like any other sportscar and full details on how to repair floor and sill areas have been covered in the restoration of the *Practical Classics* Midget which shares a virtually identical structure with that of the 'Frog'. *Practical Classics* hasn't before now, been able to show how to repair a Mk I Sprite's spring mounting points and indeed, that area of the car didn't need to be repaired when *Practical Classics* restored the 'prize' Sprite a few years ago. At my bodyshop, 'The Classic Restoration Centre'

in Worcestershire (Tel: 088 67 695) we have restored a number of Frogeyes and the following picture sequence is a sort of 'edited highlights' of some of the restorations carried out, illustrating the main points. Mk II Sprites and Mk I Midgets, the first cars with the 'Spridget' bodyshape, also used quarter-elliptics and the techniques shown here apply equally to those cars.

When you first look at the heelboard of an early Sprite or Midget (or even a later one, come to that!) it's not immediately apparent how it all goes together. The problem is that at first sight, the heelboard you can see from inside the car (it's the almost vertical, fluted sheet, behind the seat backs) appears to be the same as the one you can see from underneath. Not so! The heelboard is actually a hollow section, wider at the bottom than at the top, rather like a tall, thin Toblerone.

Lindsay Porter, author of the Haynes Sprite and Midget Restoration Guide, shows how to put life back into the 'Frogeye' (and Mk I Midget/Mk II Sprite) spring mountings.

Spridget Rebuild

After removing the fuel tank, which comes off in exactly the same way as the later Midget's tank, the axle must be removed. See the latter part of this article for details of mounting arrangements. Very badly corroded cars have been known to eject complete spring boxes without a spanner being turned. If you can dismantle the axle mountings and you haven't done so before, it's not a bad idea to go to the extra trouble so that you learn how it all goes back together, rather than simply cutting it all out with the welding torch. Also dismantle the handbrake linkage, remove check straps (or cut through if they are to be replaced), unbolt radius arms and disconnect shock absorbers and brake hydraulics. Be prepared to use heat to free the many stubborn nuts and bolts; even a butane blowtorch can help enormously, but be sure that there is nothing inflammable within range in the boot or cockpit.

This is the complete assembly with the radius arm lifted away. Note the reinforcing gusset (arrowed) to which the shock absorbers are bolted. These give vital stiffness to the rear of the car and should be left in place until after the springs have been removed, even until the outer heelboard panel has been removed (if this is necessary). It not only helps to keep the rear of the car in shape, it also gives a reference for all the new bits to be fitted, and since they will determine the alignment of the rear axle, they must be fitted properly.

Almost at each end, a reinforced box, open at the rear, is fitted between the two almost upright faces. The quarter elliptic springs (which means, in effect, that they are supported only at one end), slide into these boxes.

Underneath each box is a reinforcement plate with flanged edges which many people mistake for being the major structural support. In fact, you can't *see* the structural condition of the spring boxes at all if you haven't got x-ray vision so this is a difficult area to

Next switch to inside the cockpit and cut away as much of the heelboard inner panel as is necessary to remove the old spring box and also to remove corroded metal. Bolt the new spring box into place through the radius arm mounting (arrow 1), and temporarily through the floor (arrow 2). Ignore the holes left in the floor for fitting later-type springs (arrow 3) and either weld them up later or fit grommets.

Now that the exact position of the spring box has been established, the shock absorber mounting plate can be cut away (although in many cases it will remain sound enough to retain, being made of stouter metal) and complete the fitting up of a new heelboard outer panel. Again, in many cases this panel can be retained and simply patched at the outer edges where it tends to corrode first. This car was a shocker! Note that the whole inner wing area as well as the "chassis" box section had badly corroded.

Although firms like Spridgebits market whole spring boxes, we have made our own in the past using a carefully constructed card template as a guide. The special threaded lugs, acting like big captive nuts, were cut out of the original section and welded to the new after it had been formed.

assess, especially when buying an early Sprite or Midget. Unfortunately, it's also the hardest and most expensive part on the car to repair and so it's worthwhile examining the area carefully and also knowing what clues to look for. The first thing to check is whether

The two triangular support sections which fit either side of the spring box were also hand made on this occasion. Nothing more elaborate than a pair of strips of angle iron were used as folders and here the first fold is being 'slapped' into a sharp corner and a flat face on its topmost surface.

Reassembly is now relatively straightforward. Here the radius arm mounting is being bolted back onto the spring box through the heelboard outer panel. You can see that locating the spring box first to the radius arm mounting in its original untouched position, then fixing it temporarily to the floor, ensured that everything went back in exactly the right place.

the reinforcement plate has been welded to the rear of the floor. This is a common 'bodge' in cases where the spring mountings have shown signs of wilting. Often the external corrosion will have been plated, and the reinforcement plate welded to the floor in the mistaken belief that location to a flimsy floor pan will solve the problem. The second clue is to check the angle at which the body of the spring comes out of the heelboard outer panel as viewed from beneath. It should be perfectly horizontal where it exits from the car (although it soon curves downwards, of course); if it points upwards at all, you can be sure that the spring and spring box are collapsing under the weight of the car. Also try jacking the car with the weight off the axle and watch from floor level to see if the spring mountings move.

Having said that repairing this area is the most expensive job to carry out on the car, it's not so if you're doing the work yourself, of course. If you do decide to tackle the job yourself, be sure that you support the rear of the car in such a way that it can't sag as you cut the heelboard away. Even without the

Next the shock absorber mounting-cum-reinforcing gusset is offered up and bolted into place. You might as well put the shock absorbers back at this stage, so that the mounting bolts can be used and pulled up tight. The top edge of this Spridgebits repair panel also forms a very useful reinforcement flange.

A small but vital point when the heelboard is being replaced: It comes with holes for mounting the exhaust pipe bracket but no captive nuts. Since you can't get at the inside of the panel when it is all closed off, it makes good sense to weld or braze a couple of nuts into the inner face of the panel at this stage.

Meanwhile, back in the cockpit . . . a repair panel was made to replace the corroded metal of the inner heelboard, and is being offered up here with a new reinforcement panel. The old one had been removed by drilling out its retaining spot welds when the inner heelboard was partly cut away.

Note that the reinforcement panel has been bolted down to the pre-drilled floor pan by the front bolts only to ensure positional accuracy. The position of the holes is being marked with the drill before the repair panel (sandwiched between reinforcement and heelboard panels) was removed and drilled out properly. The reinforcement panel then bolted through to nuts welded in place on the spring box.

The next job was to slide the springs back into the spring boxes. They are held firmly in place by a U-bolt which passes over the spring at the point where the spring box is cut away (see arrow), through the base of the spring box and then through the reinforcement plate and sits underneath the floor. In this shot, the U-bolt and reinforcement plate are held there for illustrative purposes, the spring in the background being actually fitted into place.

rear axle in place, the rear of the car is a fairly heavy structure and, even sound inner and outer sills and floor won't stop it distorting as so much of the car's rear-end strength resides in those triangular-section heelboards. Ideally, the car should be supported just a little way forwards of the heelboards and also in the area of the boot floor with the weight evenly distributed. The operations are described in the picture captions.

As the last shot in the picture sequence shows, it is far easier to fit the spring without the inner heelboard in place in that area, so it obviously makes sense to weld it up only after the spring has been fitted.

Although the spring box area is of quite solid construction it does rot as is all too clear. Help to hold future corrosion back by painting liberal doses of Waxoyl into the spring box itself, especially where the spring

Two more bolts pass upwards through the sub-floor reinforcement plate, through holes in the spring and into tapped holes in the block on the end of this strange looking device which is slid into place on the top of the spring. Again, the spring has already been fitted in this shot and the mounting plate is held for illustrative purposes.

fits, as injection later probably won't penetrate that far. *Don't* get Waxoyl onto the areas where you are going to weld, however, as fresh Waxoyl is very flammable and how would you go about putting out a fire inside such a spacious but enclosed box section?

In an articlee of this length, it isn't possible to go into all the ancillary jobs such as check strap renewal, cleaning and painting the axle and renewing brake lines, but if you are going this far it would be extremely short sighted not to go the whole way and do the job properly and probably renew the springs too. One component that certainly should be replaced is the radius arm itself. It is a hollow box section made up of two steel pressings and rots as readily as the next box section. It takes quite a load from the torsional forces on the axle so needs to be in good condition, in addition to which its mounting bolts will have been almost impossible to get out and if they have been heated the rubbers in the ends of the radius arms will be ruined in any case. Check-strap mountings are invariably just as awkward and are best removed after the axle is out of the way (which means cutting through the old ones of course) and carefully easing the nuts off the mounting pins with the application of heat.

The whole job is certainly the most ambitious single repair to be carried out on a Frogeye but if you adopt a logical system of removal and replacement as shown, which ensures correct alignment of the various parts, you can make sure that your 'Frog' is sound in a crucial area and rest content that you have refreshed parts that most restorers *never* reach!

□

NEXT MONTH

Spridget front-end repairs.

Spridget Rebuild /10

As with almost any car, the chances are that if the front wings are obviously in need of replacement, whatever's underneath won't be much better when it comes to light. Lucky 'Frog' owners will know the state of their inner wings or mudguards without needing to indulge in any dismantling because they are revealed on lifting the bonnet, but Spridget owners can also get a pretty fair idea of how much rot is present in theirs, by careful poking about in the engine compartment.

In the case of the *Practical Classics* Midget, the front wings were taken off with the full expectation of major repairs or replacement and sure enough, both inner wings were suffering from corrosion in the usual places — round the outer circumferences, where they meet the bulkhead, and the top faces. They

are made from a number of fairly simple panels spot-welded together, and while the overlapping flanges which result are partly what encourage rot in the first place, when it comes to repairs it does give you the option of replacing individual sections of the inner wing rather than replacing it entirely. If you are considering repairs, however, be sure to

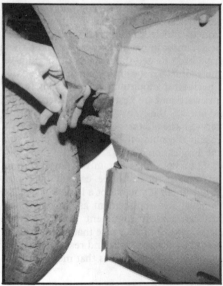

Inner front wings rot where they join the bulkhead and round the outer circumference flanges.

Body of offside inner wing being lifted clear after being freed from spot welds.

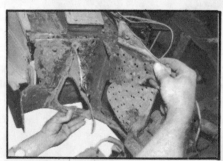

Inner wing is secured by numerous spot-welds adjacent to front suspension, each of which have to be drilled. Also seen is triangular piece which attaches to gusset.

Front inner wing fitting and repairs, and front chassis repairs are the topic this month. Paul Skilleter and Lindsay Porter take up the story on our 1969 Midget.

These removed, the rot damage in the triangulated gusset can be seen, due to it collecting mud. Note also rotted portions of bulkhead, some of which have been cut out.

This is the nearside gusset shown from inside the engine bay; the debris which forms inside can clearly be seen.

New bottom section of gusset was made, and bulkhead damaged areas trimmed away prior to patching.

The new section of gusset was let in, and the bulkhead patches welded up; here the bulkhead is being dressed at the end of the welding operations.

New Spridgebits inner front wing complete; triangle aperture has been cut out to match the original inner wing, but this might not really be a good idea.

strip the whole inner wing of paint and clean back to bright metal or you could miss pinholing disguised by dirt and scale.

Removing the outer front wings has been covered in a previous episode, and is essential to get proper access to the inner wings on a Spridget as mentioned. At this stage or shortly after, Lindsay Porter's Classic Restoration Centre also removed the front radiator

The new inner wing in position; it will eventually be welded to bulkhead and gusset, but further checks must be carried out first.

New inner wing 'boxes' triangular gusset, seating on its 'floor' and slotting between it and plate on right. Inner wing flange (left) abuts bulkhead.

or grille panel and front valance, to which each wing is also secured by five bolts. The repair of this item will be covered later. With outer wings off and the radiator out, the radiator panel can be taken off the car simply by undoing the bolts securing its tray to the projecting front chassis members (in practice this tray is usually rotten and the panel can sometimes virtually be pulled off the car).

A variety of inner wing repair sections are available from Spridgebits (who as you know are supplying nearly all the parts we need for this particular Project Car), most of them covering the top and outer portions of the wing. Or, as they are made from flat or single-curvature steel sheet, the more ambitious amongst you could make your own if you have the time and some tin-snips. Remove the sections needing replacement (by drilling and careful chiselling), make carboard templates from them, scribe the shape onto sheet steel, cut out and bend and/or fold as necessary on the bench.

Very often, though, the damage will be extensive enough to require the whole inner wing to be replaced, especially on Frog-eyes

Spridget Rebuild

This is the Spridgebits 'edge/centre section' inner wing, not quite the whole thing but covering the areas most likely to rot.

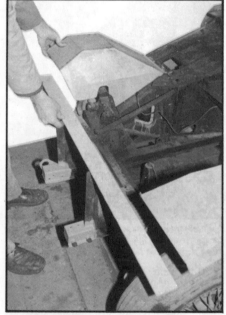

A straight-edge was used as oene guide to check 'front/rear' position of inner wings before welding commenced, using the radiator/front panel mounting uprights as the datum point.

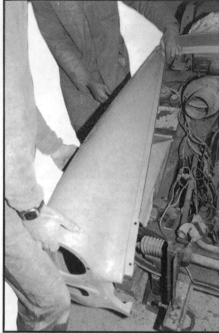

It's also advisable to offer up the front wings first, as wrongly-installed inner wings can affect these when they come to be mounted.

Spot-welding the Spridgebits 'edge/centre section' panel to the nearside after checks had been completed. Often the inner face of the wing remains good, just the centre and outer parts becoming perforated.

The offside complete inner wing being gas-welded to the top of the bulkhead.

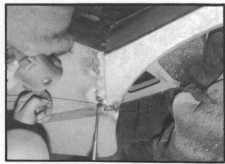

The inner wing flanges are also secured by weld to the sill, and to the bulkhead (or footwell) sides. Inside the arch, plug welds will secure it to internal mounting plate and disguise the spot-weld drillings.

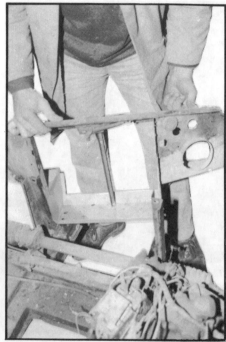

Before front edges of chassis rails can be replaced, front radiator panel needs to be unbolted. Repairs to this panel will be covered later.

Front end of chassis rails frequently corrode; note threaded tubes passing through — these carry the bumper brackets.

perhaps where all but the most perfect repairs are going to show whenever you lift the bonnet. The only difficulty associated with removing an entire front inner wing is separating it from the engine bay's triangulated gusset and adjacent plate, the latter requiring a tedious process of drilling out what seems to be hundreds of individual spot-welds. Welds also have to be broken where the inner wing meets the bulkhead.

The Spridgebits replacement inner wing fitted well, but first considerable patching and welding of the bulkhead was needed. As regular readers will know, the bulkhead (or footwell) sides had already been replaced or repaired, so this work concerned the vertical wall directly behind the inner wings. Also in this area is the gussett which triangulates

the chassis rails to the bulkhead; this in true BMC tradition is 'designed' to catch mud and consequently rots out, usually at and just above the bottom. A new section of metal had to be made to replace the damaged area, and a few other small holes had to be ground clean and filled with weld.

CONTINUED ON PAGE 56

Spridget Rebuild/11

When it comes to front wings, at least the Spridget has the bolt-on variety which makes life a bit easier; we've already covered their removal, and this month the topic centres around their repair.

As with most cars, the Spridget wings are vunerable to both rust and accident damage, and need to be entirely stripped of paint, dirt and old filler so that their condition can be properly assessed. It may well be that unless you are working to a very tight budget, the amount of time and effort needed to bring poor wings up to scratch may not be worthwhile and the best course of action is then to throw them away and buy new ones — these are now quite readily available for the various types of Spidget (sidelight mountings changed for example), albeit at a cost of around £75 each.

In fact Lindsay's Classic Restoration Centre opted for new wings from our suppliers, Spridgebits, but first carried out repairs to the original front wings to show what is involved. On stripping the wings you'll probably find rust damage along the mounting flanges, at the front of the wing, and (especially) along the bottoms of the wing 'sides'. For the latter repair sections are available, and one is shown being fitted in the picture sequences.

Needless to say it's essential to take very great care in fitting such a section, because if you get it wrong it's going to show. Leave a generous overlap between wing and repair section when you cut these to match, and you might find offering up the opposite-side wing 'mirror-fashion', as in the pictures, one method of positioning the repair section accurately. Whatever you do, don't permanently weld the patch in until you've refitted the wings to the car, preferably in conjunction with the bonnet so you can obtain the

Front wing repairs bring the saga of the Midget's body rebuild near to its conclusion. Paul Skilleter and Lindsay Porter continue the story.

Spridget Rebuild

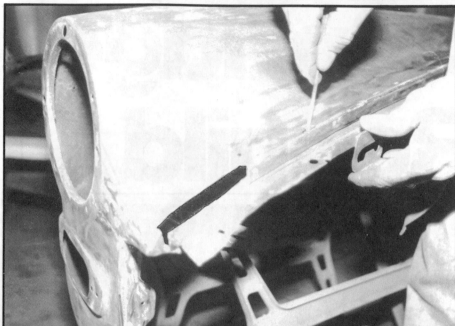

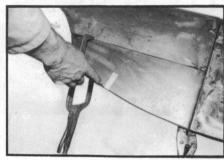

Serious rot often affects the lower side part of a Spridget front wing; here a repair section has been tacked into place, positioned with the aid of the opposite-side wing (right) being placed end-to-end with it.

Spridget front wings rot in a number of places — here a section of the mounting flange has had to be cut out, while pin-holing extends further up the wing as can be seen.

This is the same area repaired; a suitable patch was made up, shaped to match the wing's contour, welded in and lead-loaded.

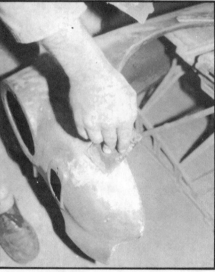

Minor dents were beaten out, linished and filled.

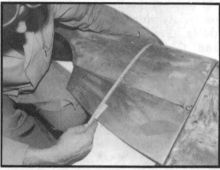

A further reference point mid-way along the repair section was marked, and then measured with a steel tape . . .

. . . which was then transferred to the other front wing (original at that point) to make sure it was the same. Other wing is also being given a (smaller) repair section in this area.

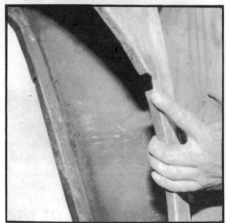

The wheel-arch flanges may need attention too — here a small section of rot has been cut out, ready for a new piece of steel to be let-in.

best fit between all three and the bulkhead/hinge pillar.

Fitting Spridget front wings is, in any case, a rather more fraught procedure than with most cars, for the simple reason that the rear of the wing doesn't end in a door gap (where you can also have a door to play around with) but at the immovable hinge pillar. As the photograph shows, on our car the bonnet projected too far forward — it had probably been like this when we first got the car but in the general mess it wasn't noticeable. Hence another good reason for opting for new front wings altogether.

Incidentally, when looking for new or better secondhand wings, do make sure you get the right type — Sprite wings for instance

Prior to mounting the wing, fixing holes had to be drilled in side footwell panel, these not being included on the repair section installed there.

The wing, complete with repair section only temporarily attached, was positioned on car.

Repair section could then be moved until the best fit with sill and hinge pillar was obtained.

Only then was the section MIG welded into place. Note that welding across such a relatively wide area of metal can result in distortion — the MIG equipment minimises this danger but even then only spot and not continuous welds were used.

The join was linished then lead-loaded; good-quality plastic filler would be a perfectly accepted alternative however.

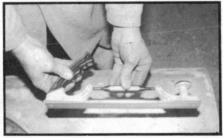

This is a Sykes Pickavant file with screw adjustment to alter curvature of special flexible file; for this job it was set to a slight convex curve so the corners of the file wouldn't dig in.

The primered wing on the car for a further trial-fit; bolts were not tightened at this stage, as whatever movement was possible would be useful in lining-up with the bonnet.

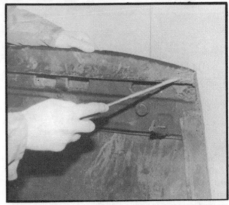

Bonnet repair: our car's was amazingly sound, but there was still some rot at the corners. Normally you can expect holes wherever there's double-skinning especially at front and rear.

Section of steel was cut to generously match area of rot removed, tacked down, heated and then stretched and bent to conform to the right shape.

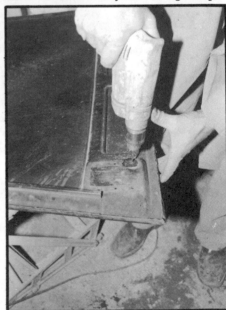

Other details needed attending to, such as drilling out stud which had sheared on removal of bonnet from car.

Spridget Rebuild

Hole was then re-tapped, using plug or bottoming tap which is parallel down its entire length, rather then tapered tap which would have to be wound down a long way and might damage outer skin of bonnet.

have no holes for the decorative side-strip, and the sidelight apertures differed after October 1969 when they were lowered.

Our Midget is some way ahead of these features, you'll be pleased to hear; the suspension and brakes have been overhauled, the shell has been painted, all the trim parts are being assembled ready for fitting-up, and the 1275cc engine rebuilt. The completion did, in fact, only just miss the Bromley Pageant date in June and we should soon be able to show you a picture of the finished car. But

Bonnet was refitted to car and an attempt made to line it up with wings. Here it's being eased forward slightly to clear scuttle.

we've decided in the meantime to continue with the in-depth features, which will be covering all the important aspects mentioned above over the next few issues.

> ## NEXT MONTH
> Final front-end repairs,
> and rear axle work.

Problem: bonnet would always protrude beyond wings no matter what. Cause undoubtedly lay with original wings rather than bonnet and was eventually countered by fitting new wings.

Meanwhile, with wings and bonnet removed again, car was turned over so that underside could be finally cleaned, checked, sealed and painted.

Spridget Rebuild/12

During and after the body rebuild, all the car's suspension componets were removed for reconditioning as necessary, and this of course included the rear axle. The basics of the job are followed in the pictures, though if you want the fine detail, we recommend a good workshop manual like the Haynes Sprite/Midget publication.

However, in real life things don't always work out as easily as manuals can imply, and the main point to bear in mind when tackling a rear axle is that this particular component is totally exposed and is attacked by the elements in a big way — and just about everything removable on it tends to rust and seize up over the years and the miles. Getting the axle off the car is usually the easy bit; stripping it afterwards is usually much harder work!

It's important not to be heavy-handed though when you come up against seized nuts, especially where they are on captive bolts or studs which, if damaged, may be very difficult to replace — particularly as on applications such as this, the chances are they aren't standard bolts and sometimes have special shanks and so on. A source of heat is usually necessary, but for a start, apply releasing fluid a good 24 hours before you begin work.

However, releasing fluid doesn't always do the trick and heat usually has to be resorted to as the next step, the flame expanding the nut away from the rust and breaking the seal. Obviously a gas torch is best because it supplies a very concentrated and fairly localised source of heat, but don't depise the humble butane lamp which can do the job almost as well. It goes without saying, of course, that you must never use an open flame near a petrol tank — and that includes that empty one left in the corner of the garage. It shouldn't be there — get it outside or in the garden shed well away from any naked

A digression from bodywork this month as we cover the renovation of the rear axle on our '69 Midget.

Spridget Rebuild

Axle should be supported on jack under diff., and assuming propshaft, damper link, brakes etc have been disconnected, rear spring shackle can be removed.

Spring was removed from axle by undoing 'U' bolt nuts, a nice easy job with the unit off the car.

lights or cigarettes, as potentially it makes a very fine bomb.

It's a fact that on such as a rear axle, many of the stubborn nuts will be near rubber bushed components; this is no bother if you're embarking on a truly thorough restoration as we are, because all such rubbers will be replaced anyway — in that case, all they represent is a source of rather smelly smoke, and you should keep a squeezy bottle nearby to douse any small fires which break out. If you don't intend to replace said rubber, protect it with wet rags or other forms of heat shield. Alternatively — and this may become necessary anyway — drill and then

Front end of spring is hidden up in bulkhead and so has to be taken off complete with shackle bracket which is bolted to the floor.

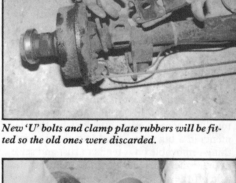

New 'U' bolts and clamp plate rubbers will be fitted so the old ones were discarded.

carefully chisel the offending nuts away.

A lot of people don't associate back axles with rot, but in the case of cars which have been on the road for a long time, rust can in fact attack axle bracketry and mountings as badly as it does bodywork. We therefore examined our Midget's axle carefully during the cleaning-down procedure, and sure enough found holes in the bump-stop mounting boxes. Lindsay Porter contemplated repairing them, but in view of the cheap and plentiful supply of second-hand axles, elected to ask our suppliers Spridgebits for a good used replacement.

Check straps were to be renewed so were cut through, allowing axle to be wheeled out from under car.

Remains of check strap being cut off (use a Stanley knife — and to prevent binding, have a cup of water handy to wet the knife which then slides easily).

Work could now begin on freeing the front shackle plate; heat was essential for removal of the shackle pin itself.

These are the component parts; new shackles (or hanger) plates are available if required, so are all bolts.

Bump stop rubber can just be pulled off its mushroom-type mounting.

With all rubber out of the way, heat can be used to help shift check strap mounting bolt.

Unprotected from the elements, bump stop housing is prone to rot, shown up on our axle by a few taps with the hammer.

Handbrake linkage was detached from backplate lever by removing pin.

The handbrake compensator mounting nuts required careful drilling then chiselling — they'd seized but it was important not to damage threads.

The compensator unit showed extreme wear, quite enough to prevent the handbrake working properly even if everything was apparently adjusted correctly.

Work commenced on scraping and disc sanding the stripped axle casing free of mud and scale prior to painting.

It was this replacement unit then which was thoroughly cleaned and partially dismantled for checking over. So far as the cleaning part went, we decided against sand-blasting because of the known possibility of the sand getting into the diff. assembly so it was done by hand. The rust scale was so thick a wire brush or even the linisher skated over the surface so in the end it was a case of getting down to it with scrapers and an old wood chisel. Only then could the linisher be usefully brought into action to get back to bright

When basically clean, drums, backplates, hub bearings and half-shafts were removed for inspection, and for replacement of oil seals. A hub puller is needed for this operation of course.

Bearing was rinsed in clean petrol and spun to detect 'grittyness' or wear.

All individual components were cleaned and painted.

metal. Anti-rust primer was followed by black enamel, brushed on. Care was taken to Waxoyl all brackets and those bump stop boxes too.

Brakes are a subject we'll be returning to, but as can be seen the handbrake linkage was found to be in a bad way, particularly the compensator unit fitted to this age of Spridget. The thing to do here is replace the

Spridget Rebuild

unit altogether, but it could have been repaired by welding up the worn parts and re-drilling, and reassembling with all new split pins, clevis pins, felt pads, nuts and bolts. □

Backplate and rear brakes were reassembled on the cleaned and painted axle.

New hub and bearing assemblies were eventually fitted to our axle; also shown are the relined rear brake shoes and new wheel cylinder.

NEXT MONTH
Front suspension rebuild.

Spridget Rebuild/13

Needless to say, we want our Project Car Midget to handle like a new car and not just look like one, and so a complete rebuild of the front suspension was a 'must'. This is a fairly complex job and not exactly cheap, so although we've covered this topic before (in features on the A35 and A40, which share the same basic set-up) it will more than bear repeating — and expanding on — especially as in the two years since we last talked about this suspension we've gathered a lot more readers.

First of all you will want to check on exactly what needs replacing, as although we've renewed every wearing part this isn't always necessary. Start by jacking the front wheels clear of the ground; then hold a wheel at top and bottom and attempt to 'rock' it. If movement is evident, trace it back (while continuing to rock the wheel) to the damper link/trunnion rubber bushes, or to the inner wishbone mounting rubbers, or to the swivel pin (kingpin) and its metal bushes. Frankly, the typical elderly Spridget usually needs the whole lot doing, so don't be too hopeful about limiting the work.

Having disconnected steering tie-rod from arm (left), disc brake can be unbolted; this can be tied up out of the way without disturbing hydraulics if no brake work is needed.

Tools You Need

9/16" and 1/2" AF sockets and spanners; Philips and plain screwdrivers; ball joint splitter; soft hammer; drift; jack; axle stands; and possibly drill and cold chisel!!

The Spridget-type suspension not only wears in the places mentioned, but can be inordinately difficult to take apart — notably when it comes to detaching the swivel pin from the fulcrum pin which hinges the outer ends of the wishbone, and also the wishbone itself from the car. So much so that many people find it easier to take advantage of the exchange schemes offered by specialists like Spridgebits, whereby you simply swop your wishbone and swivel pin complete for a rebuilt assembly. Especially since (a) you will very likely have to order an exchange wishbone anyway, as the fulcrum pin seizes in it, and (b) unless you have a reamer you won't be able to fit a new swivel pin and bushes to your stub axle.

The pictures show the suspension being relieved of the stub axle hub assembly, and the road spring, plus the wishbones and swivel pin being detached from the car as a unit for an exchange of the sort discussed. However, if you do intend fitting a new swivel pin kit yourself, here's some tips on how to remove a recalcitrant pin.

The lower fulcrum pin has threaded ends which turn in the wishbone to accommodate

Overhauling the front suspension. Paul Skilleter brings you the story — which is also very relevent to A30/A35 and A40 owners. Photographs by Lindsay Porter.

49

Spridget Rebuild

With the jack taking the damper arm off rubber pad (without obstructing axle assembly), pinchbolt is undone at end of arm, nut unscrewed from threaded end of trunnion (A, already off) and finally castellated nut B (split-pinned) from swivel pin where it protrudes through trunnion.

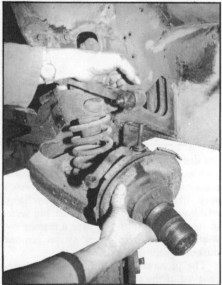

Trunnion is tapped from underneath so that it and damper arm pull off swivel pin (or kingpin) – being careful to catch hub assembly as it's released.

suspension movement. Often, through lack of grease or age, these wear the threads in the wishbone requiring it to be professionally reconditioned, and/or seizing solid at the same time. This makes removing the fulcrum pin in the conventional manner (by applying a screw driver to its slotted end and unscrewing it) impossible; so how do you remove it and thus release the swivel pin?

Top trunnion itself can then be tapped free.

At this stage the hub assembly can be slid from swivel pin.

Well, first of course you have to remove the cotter pin which passes through the boss of the swivel pin and bears on a 'flat' on the fulcrum pin, (so that the two move together). Not so easy as it sounds – you may get the nut off but usually the pin itself seizes inside the boss, and hammering it merely spreads the threaded end making it even more difficult to push through. What you have to do, therefore, is chisel the cotter pin neatly off flush at

If required, damper can now be unbolted from chassis.

its base, and as the end now can't spread,, it can be drifted out with a suitable length of rod.

But if nothing seems to shift the fulcrum pin itself, dramatic tactics are required. Since the swivel pin is to be scrapped anyway, the technique evolved by our Terry Bramhall is to drill four or five holes in the swivel pin boss (let the stub axle swing downwards, and attack the part of the swivel pin left at the top), then apply the cold chisel until the metal seperates and allows the swivel pin to come away from the fulcrum pin. The latter

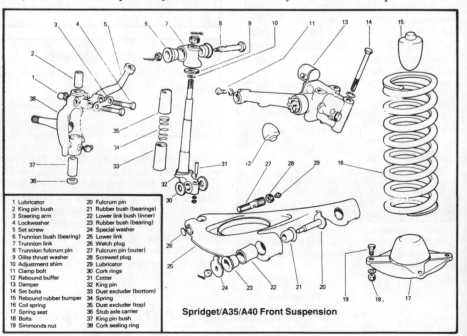

1 Lubricator	20 Fulcrum pin
2 King pin bush	21 Rubber bush (bearings)
3 Steering arm	22 Lower link bush (inner)
4 Lockwasher	23 Rubber bush (bearing)
5 Set screw	24 Special washer
6 Trunnion bush (bearing)	25 Lower link
7 Trunnion link	26 Welch plug
8 Trunnion fulcrum pin	27 Fulcrum pin (outer)
9 Oilite thrust washer	28 Screwed plug
10 Adjustment shim	29 Lubricator
11 Clamp bolt	30 Cork rings
12 Rebound buffer	31 Cotter
13 Damper	32 King pin
14 Set bolts	33 Dust excluder (bottom)
15 Rebound rubber bumper	34 Spring
16 Coil spring	35 Dust excluder (top)
17 Spring seat	36 Stub axle carrier
18 Bolts	37 King pin bush
19 Simmonds nut	38 Cork sealing ring

Spridget/A35/A40 Front Suspension

Very slowly, and keeping car (supported on stands) between you and it, wishbone can be lowered on jack until spring is completely decompressed. Only then should spring seat be unbolted as shown here.

Spring is dropped out; note seat on floor.

Wishbone is released by (theoretically) undoing castellated nuts securing fulcrum pins and drifting them out – or if stubborn, using wedge-type ball joint splitter between special washer (indicated) and mounting may do the job.

Often though, one or more pins seize solid in bushes, and on the offside of our car, one had to be cut off with an angle grinder to get wishbone away from car.

Axle assembly was dismantled on bench and steering arm, and hub dismantled (puller is needed for latter). Sprung mud-shield assembly should be retained and cleaned as new ones are not currently available.

can then be wound out using a spanner on the convenient 'flat'.

Next, a word about road springs. The Spridget may be a small car but its coil springs still contain an enormous amount of energy when compressed. This means that a spring compressor must be used on some cars, though in the case of our Midget, having detached the top trunnion from the damper link, you can allow the supporting jack under the lower wishbone to gradually descend until all the tension has been taken out of the spring. Whatever you do, don't attempt to unbolt the spring plate while the spring is under compression; and if you are in doubt, use a spring compressor or get a gar-

Bump-stop and rebound rubbers are positioned as the first step on re-assembly (just to confuse you, this sequence is followed on the offside suspension).

Here, the new fulcrum pin is assembled on wishbone; first, hold cork sealing rings in wishbone with grease.

Insert swivel pin boss and thread fulcrum pin into wishbone, having greased everything well first.

age to do this particular job – springs are dangerous!

On the subject of replacement parts, you have a wide choice ranging from a complete axle set which includes wishbones and kingpins for both sides, all fully rebuilt, for around £75, to just kingpin kits on their own (which require reaming of the bushes when fitting to your original stub axles). Plus the Metallastic bushes for the inner wishbone mountings, their pins, and virtually all individiual bushes, washers, cork seals and the top trunnion shims. You will probably find the list of parts in this month's Spridgebits advertisement a help in sorting out what you need – they supplied us with all the parts used on our car.

In addition, we fitted reconditioned dam-

Spridget Rebuild

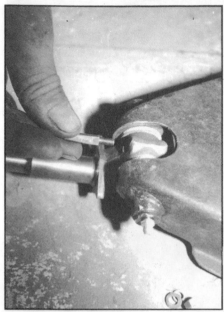

Next the cotter pin which prevents swivel pin turning on shaft is pushed home, having made sure that rebate on shaft is lined up with cotter pin holes; its nut and washers are then replaced.

Here the dust excluder tubes have been inserted into stub axle carrier, and the sealing ring is being fitted.

Stub axle (well greased) is slid over swivel pin, followed by phospher bronze thrust washer, shims if necessary, and trunnion.

Now the wishbone itself can be attached to the car. This picture shows the bushes, pin and special washers used to do the job.

Wishbone is offered up to mounting points, rubber bushes pushed in from either side (if stiff, a little hydraulic fluid helps), pins and washers inserted, followed by nuts and split-pins – or (new) Nyloc nuts on some cars.

With trunnion bolted down, there should be some resistance on turning the stub axle lock to lock, but no vertical movement; adjust with shims if necessary. Pin and Metallastic bushes for damper arm are also shown.

Without any spring to worry about, top trunnion is easily lined up with damper arm, the relevant bushes and washers inserted, followed by fulcrum pin and its split-pinned nut. Don't forget pinch-bolt, shown here.

Road spring is inserted through wishbones from below, with spring pan under.

CONTINUED ON PAGE 56

Spridget Rebuild/14

This instalment is something in the nature of a flash-back, as the car itself is now having its engine put back and may even have moved under its own steam by the time you read this. But while in the August issue we covered front wing repair — and, to an extent, refitting — we mentioned then that the Midget was actually destined to receive brand-new front wings, and this is what we're going to talk about this month.

As we also mentioned before, most elderly Spridgets will need repairs or replacements for the *inner* front wings too if the outer ones are so far gone as to need throwing away, and an important point to make here is that the new inner wings should just be tacked into position at first, and the outer front wings tried. This is because it's possible for them to foul, and they may have to be moved slightly.

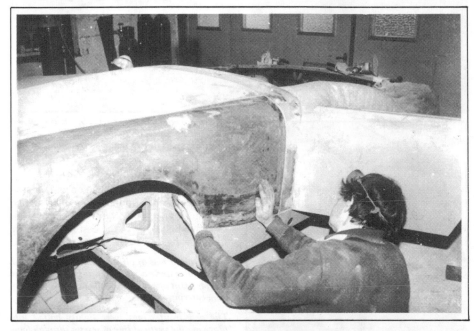

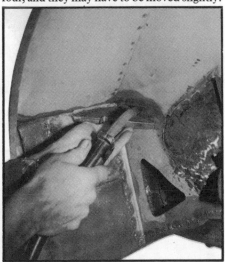

The complete new front inner wing panel came without fixtures and fittings, such as this gusset plate which had to be welded in. Front wings should be offered up before finally welding inner wings in place.

Note, however, that the gap (invisible fortunately from outside the car) between inner and outer front wings does not appear to be either particularly close or consistent, often narrowing towards the front, and there doesn't seem to be much you can do about it, short of being fanatical and re-shaping the entire inner wings to suit.

The front panel assembly is also positioned at this stage, again experimentally; this is where those who are doing a complete rebuild score, as with all front-end panel-work offered up loosely, everything can be moved around to achieve the optimum fit. Outer panels can be removed when this has been achieved (don't forget to trial-fit the bonnet too) and the inner wings and engine bay cleaned, prepared, and sprayed with primer. A colour coat could also be applied to this same area now if desired.

Getting the front outer wings to fit properly is the most important aspect of the whole job, and with the Spridget you have the disadvantage of the rear of the wings abutting not movable doors, like with most cars, but immovable hinge pillars. Thus you can't pack the door hinges out or anything to help you obtain the right gaps there. All must be

It's worthwhile checking before primering the engine bay to make sure no more minor repairs are needed — here, the mounting bracket for coil had lost a captive nut and a new one had to be brazed on — not something to do with nice new paint all around.

Fitting new front wings and re-installing the front panel. Paul Skilleter continues the story of our 1969 Midget.

Spridget Rebuild

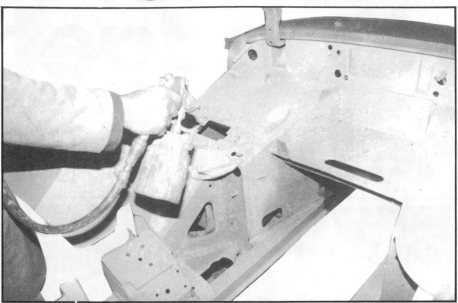

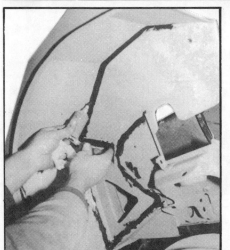

After thorough cleaning, engine bay was sprayed with primer then high-build primer filler, which afterwards was flatted ready for the colour coats.

achieved by moving the wings themselves, and be prepared to take them on and off several times to open up mounting holes and so on. The bonnet too will probably have to be moved to help achieve the best fit between it and the wings. Even then you are unlikely to

Before colour was applied, seam sealer was used on all seams and overlaps; it remains flexible but accepts paint afterwards, while preventing water from entering seams.

The new front wings were lightly bolted into place via the vertical line of screws through footwell sides and ends of bulkhead drain guttering. Front panel was offered up and bolted to fronts of wings, again without tightening up.

The undertray of front panel bolts onto chassis legs (two each side). A new 'pattern' part, stamped holes in tray needed opening out a little to allow front panel to fit properly.

achieve perfection (but let's face it, a Spridget fresh from the factory was never perfect either!) and you may have to compromise to an extent. At the least, however, try and make gaps parallel even if they are not identical side-to-side. One small ray of hope

The front valance panel is offered up next; its curvature had to be altered to conform to that of the wings, and held in position while being welded to front panel — a two-man job.

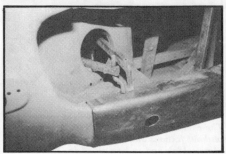

Having been tacked in place with MIG welder, the spot-welder was used from inside front wing to additionally secure valance to front panel. Valance is also bolted (two per side) to vertical flange of front wings.

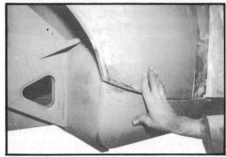

Crucial points to watch when fitting the front wings are along sill, 'A' post (hinge pillar), and bonnet gaps. You may not be able to obtain a perfect result, but aim at least to get even or parallel gaps.

as you struggle is the knowledge that small discrepancies look worse when the panels are in primer than when sprayed up!

The front panel and its valance are about the last to be welded in place. Lindsay Porter (in whose small workshop the body rebuild is being done) found that the last-named required a bit of persuasion to fit, but it should be remembered that even when genuine factory panels are used, you must never expect everything to slot into place like precision engine parts — body shells just aren't made that way, and there is some truth in the theory that during construction at the factory, unitary bodyshells are put together under stress, the panels being made to conform by the massive jigs used. While this can't be used to excuse poor reproduction panels (and there are some of those about), it may possibly explain why varying degrees of persuasion are needed during the re-assembly of a body. Our major suppliers, Spridgebits, try and stock original BL panels whenever possible, or failing that the best reproduction items, many of which they have commissioned themselves.

Finally, a few notes on steering rack removal which we didn't have room for when we covered the front suspension rebuild in the October issue. Here, procedures vary though on all cars you need to support the

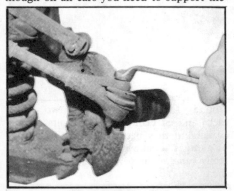

Steering rack removal: remove split pin and slotted nut on tie-rod ball joints, and tap (or separate) them from steering arms.

Release nut and bolt from clamp on lower end of steering column and scribe marks on clamp to help during reassembly.

The setscrews holding the rack brackets to the front cross-member are undone next.

The rack can now be lifted away complete; all is very accessible at this stage of a body rebuild of course — with an assembled car there's not so much room, but only the radiator has to be removed.

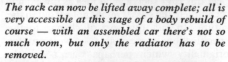

Rack can be stripped of its brackets on the bench; note packing piece (available in different thicknesses) through which rack is attached to chassis members.

front of the car on stands, remove the road wheels, and centralise the steering before you begin. The removal itself is as shown in the pictures, but apart from Mk III Midget GAN5-114643 on and all 1500cc cars there is a particular re-alignment procedure which should be followed on reassembly. This is where a conventional workshop manual comes in handy, and we ourselves make recourse to the Haynes item which covers all Spridgets from 1958 to 1980. As we've said before, this manual and Lindsay Porter's own Spridget Restoration Guide (from Haynes too) are useful to refer to in conjunction with our own rebuild articles. □

NEXT MONTH
A 'home respray' for our Midget.

CONTINUED FROM PAGE 40

Spridget Rebuild

New section was folded to replace the corroded length, with end-plate welded on and also the nuts which will take the bolts from the front panel/air intake tray.

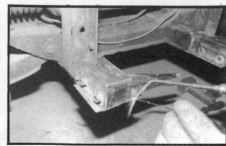

Here the new extensions are being welded on, having been fitted with their tubes. Recently Spridgebits added this chassis repair section to their range.

The outer wall of the gusset is actually formed by the inner wing, which has a matching cut-out in it as original to allow the aforementioned mud to get in. The Spridgebits replacement inner wing comes without this cut-out, but working to a policy of originality, Lindsay had the relevant area cut away. However, as he says, "in restrospect this isn't such a good idea as if we'd left it complete the gusset might not rot out in the future. In fact this sort of change to the specification is acceptable — we went for originality which perhaps wasn't entirely necessary or desirable in this case". But with

the way we intend to rust-proof the car, I don't think it very likely the rot that is going to be a serious problem with this particular Midget!

Having prepared the shell properly, stripping off all the remains of the old inner wing, the replacement was tried up. It's important to line it up correctly and to help with this, the Classic Restoration Centre used a straight-edge placed across the front of the car. It is also highly advisable to next try on the outer wings; the inners can foul these and prevent them fitting properly if not correctly installed, something you don't want to dis-

cover after welding them solidly in place! Use self-tappers or light tack-welds to locate the inner wings while these checks are carried out.

The final job covered this month is the replacement of the front four inches or so of the chassis rails. Completely enclosed box sections, as they tend to rot out quickly and thus get on the list of things to do during a restoration. Lindsay's man fabricated the part for our car, but shortly afterwards Spridgebits added the item to their list of reproduction parts so you can now buy them off-the-shelf. Incidentally, talking about parts, note that when ordering inner wings, they differ slightly from car to car — Frogeyes have a turned-under outer flange, all later cars have one which turns outwards, so make sure you end up with the correct one. As for the chassis rail repair, fitting the new extensions is not difficult but they must of course be aligned correctly. Therefore, if replacing both do one at a time leaving the original to check against and take measurements from.

NEXT MONTH
Outer wing fitting and other front-end topics.

CONTINUED FROM PAGE 52

Jack is placed under spring pan and is used to compress it until spring pan bolts can be replaced. Other assemblies can then be added including dust shield, new disc and hub.

The completed nearside suspension with steering rack connected – except that top trunnion has been fitted the wrong way round, giving massive positive camber! We did it on purpose, but Spridgebits have actually been phoned by excited customers complaining they've been sent the wrong parts…!

Here the new caliper is about to be bolted in position.

pers (but watch the very cheap ones as they may not last long) and track rod ends. Then some cars with this suspension have anti-roll bars; if so, the mounting rubbers (two,

around £1.25 pair), link arms (two, £6.80 each) and all clamps, chassis bolts etc are available if they need renewing. That's the nice things about Spridgets these days – you really can get the parts, or at least most of them. □

NEXT MONTH
Steering rack change and fitting front valance and new wings.

Respraying At Home

If, like us with our Project Car Midget, you have finally completed your body rebuild and the car is sitting there with all its new and repaired panels, you are faced with having to make a decision. Knowing all too well that it's the paint finish which people are going to see and comment on — not all your painstaking welding underneath — do you carry bravely on in the confines of your own garage and respray the car yourself, or do you take it to a professional? Of course, if you're working to a strict budget you may not have the (probably) several hundred pounds necessary to follow the second course of action; but even if you have, maybe you want to say when it's all over, "yes, I did everything myself, even the paint..." There's a great deal of satisfaction in this!

All things are possible, and a good number of the top-flight concours cars you see at rallies have been painted by their owners; but without wanting to sound pessimistic, a first-class paint job is not achieved without much effort, time and energy, even when starting out with the ideal — a body shell in bare metal with lots of nice straight, new panels on it. On the plus side however, you don't need lots of expensive equipment, and dedication and time will compensate for the expertise of a professional to a very large extent.

As a general rule, it is best to start by stripping the shell to bare metal, because only then can you tell what's underneath; however, it is feasible to merely flat good, firmly-adhering original paintwork on, say the roof and if time is a consideration, you'll save a lot of it this way, and be able to take advantage of the manufacturer's surface preparation and priming. Before even starting the job though, be sure to thoroughly wipe the paintwork — and bare metal come to that — with a spirit wipe to remove all traces of silicones (the biggest enemy of the painter) and oil or grease. Then proceed with the flatting.

Normally this is carried out using wet-and-dry paper and water, ending up with a fine grade. Production paper can be used instead but is probably a little more expensive for the amateur as it wears out quicker; the advantage is that you don't use water with it, so that unpainted metal doesn't rust, and (especially in winter months) water doesn't get into seams where it can be blown out during the subsequent spraying operations.

Our respray was carried out using cellulose

paint, as the modern acrylic two-pack paints aren't generally suitable for home use since they contain cyanides. The materials used were supplied by International, one of the largest paint manufacturers, but whatever make you choose, take the time to study the relevant application sheet (which the factor should be able to give you). This will advise you on what type of primers and primer fillers to use, and whether an isolator is advisable (this is a special 'sealer' paint applied over previously painted surfaces to prevent a reaction with the new paint, though it isn't always successful). Also, the sheet will contain notes on temperatures, drying times, mixing procedures etc – and as the data can vary between manufacturers, make sure you have the correct literature for the brand you're using. Finally, don't skimp on the thinners – buy a good quality one, not just the cheapest.

Paint is now quite a costly item, and you

will have to pay anything from £2.50 upwards per litre, with thinners costing about £8 for 5 litres. Material costs for a full repaint will therefore set you back £30-£65 or even more, depending on the size of your car and how many coats you apply. The

Spridget Rebuild/15

The paint finish should be the crowning glory of a rebuild — but is a respray feasible to tackle at home? We take a look at the techniques and the problems!

Respraying At Home

Preparing the metal: all surfaces are flatted, mostly with a block and wet-and-dry, and including what's termed 'transport primer' on new steel panels.

Now is the time to search out and fill any minor dents remaining after body repairs. Plastic filler is easier than lead to use.

Filler can be contoured with file, then finished with block.

Larger areas can be tackled with an orbital sander such as this Black and Decker; it is excellent for feathering edges where there is an overlap of filler and paint. The hand is a very sensitive instrument for assessing curvatures.

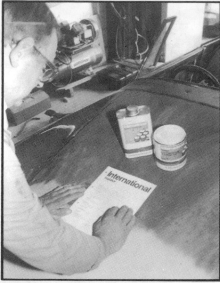

Before applying any paint, study the literature! Not all paint systems follow the same procedure so learn what the manufacturer recommends.

Final task before applying any paint is to use spirit wipe to remove any silicone, wax or grease.

Here the first coat of primer is being applied, in two thin coats. Note that underbonnet area has already been finished and is masked off.

spraygun itself need not be exotic; we used an SIP Jet 30 which comes with its own little compressor. While high quality equipment cuts down time by applying the paint more perfectly, it is true to say that if you're prepared to put the work in cutting back afterwards, you can use a Flit gun to put the paint on and still end up with a concours finish!

A word about stopper: the traditional type is cellulose based, and has the disadvantage of being slow to harden and with a tendency to shrink as it does so. Better results can be obtained by using a two-pack stopper, which is of a very fine constituency and hardens by chemical reaction, not by evaporation of a solvent. High-build primer-fillers are now widely used but don't expect them to work miracles on blemished panels — you'll still need to go through the filling and stopping stages.

The guide coat is a very important aid in achieving a good result, and overcomes the problem of the matt-surfaced primer disguising dents, ripples and other small imperfections. These are usually revealed by a light gloss colour coat 'dusted' on all over the body, enough to virtually cover the primer. Firstly it will make visible imperfections you might have missed before; then, as you block it, high and low spots will immediately be shown up as the primer shows through (or the guide coat remains in the case of depressions). You can then re-fill or stop the problem areas, and re-prime.

When at last you come to apply the first colour coats, try and choose a reasonably warm, dry day — if you apply cellulose late in the afternoon in a cold garage, your efforts can be spoiled by 'blooming', where the paint goes matt in places due to condensation. However, this and orange peel can be eradicated by blocking out with 1200 grit wet-and-

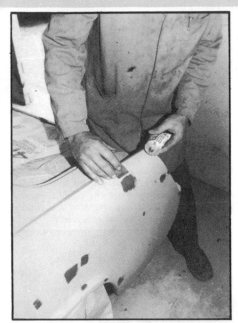

You will undoubtedly find various blemishes in the primer or primer filler, especially where a panel has been filled, and these can be countered by stopper.

When dry, the stopped areas and the whole primered body is flatted. Note how flats of fingers and ball of hand are used, giving a more even pressure than just the finger tips.

dry followed by rubbing (or polishing) compound; runs can be tackled in this way too. This incidentally is one reason why we don't recommend the use of oil paints on cars — they take months to harden properly to allow blocking, and anyway, their increased 'touch dry' time attracts dust.

Apply your top coat around all the complex areas of the body first; that is, the under curvature of the sills and wings, around mouldings and headlights and similar, before moving on to cover the large expanses of metal, working (preferably) from one corner of the car. This will avoid a dry overspray on these larger areas, which will happen if you have to go back and blow in from awkward angles the bits not covered at the first pass.

Next, a guide coat of gloss colour is applied over the whole shell; this will (literally) highlight imperfections.

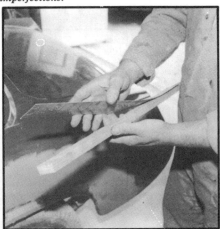

The various flatting stages, including after the guide coat, will be made more effective if you use the same long strips of self-adhesive abrasive paper as the professionals. To avoid the cost (£7-£8) of a proper holder, a length of wood can be used instead.

Here it is in action; the length more readily shows up high spots and also speeds up the work.

It's hard to prevent this from happening entirely though, but don't worry as overspray can be polished out satisfactorily. Aim to build up some four or five coats of cellulose, as this will give you a good margin for blocking out any defects or flat areas.

The trouble is, your problems don't necessarily end when you've got those top coats on. At first glance the car may look great, but now you must examine minutely every square inch, glancing along the sides and top of the bodywork so the paint catches the light and reveals faults — for some reason, strong strip lights seem to show up faults well, though nothing compensates for pushing the car outside and taking a good look at it in strong sunlight. Then, what previously appeared to be a superb result often looks rather second-rate, as patches of orange peel, runs, craters, under-surface reaction and (perhaps most common of all after orange-peel), 'rings' from insufficiently feathered old paintwork or filler literally come to light. This is a test of your dedication, because if you really want the best you'll now have to tackle each of these faults, even if it means virtually starting again.

On the subject of a reaction under the paint, this may be due to paint stripper not being washed off properly or solvents in the new paint affecting the old. To eradicate the problem you will almost certainly have to go back to bright metal, maybe applying a sealer or isolator coat as well. Where you've had to take paint off, remember to feather the edges well out before you re-apply paint otherwise you'll end up with those tell-tale rings. About the most common mistake made by amateur refinishers is limiting the area being worked on too much. Look at the way the profes-

Respraying At Home

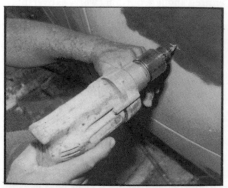

Before any top coats are applied, check that all holes for external fixtures are present; drill them in new panels if not.

It's also a good idea to actually fit some of these, to make sure everything lines up correctly; alterations to mounting holes etc. will be that much more difficult if done after the final coats of colour have been put on.

A final spirit wipe before the first coat is applied is a worthwhile precaution; it also removes any dust left over from the wash-down.

sional does it when carrying out a repair — the damage may look as if it's confined to a couple of square inches, but he will take the paint back several square feet. This enables him to blend in the repaired area successfully afterwards.

Finally, a word about conditions: it is quite possible to spray cellulose in low temperatures so long as you avoid condensation afterwards, but ideally try and bring the garage up to 65 deg. or thereabouts beforehand. As paint solvents are inflammaable, don't use an ordinary electric fire (or at the very least, unplug it before you start mixing the paint); a fan heater is much safer. The use of a calor gas fire isn't recommended for the same reason, and these also produce water vapour

At last, the first colour coat goes on! Always a morale-boosting stage, but it doesn't mean the end is near . . .

After allowing the correct drying time, the first colour coat can be flatted and examined for blemishes.

You'll almost certainly find some areas where 'rings' produced by filled areas show up, or discover small dents or ripples made all too obvious by the high gloss.

If you're really after the best job, then however you might feel inhibited by the shining new paint, these problem areas must be tackled by getting back to, if necessary, bare metal and re-filling, stopping and flatting all over again.

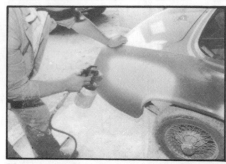

The area will need to be spot primed, with the gun set to give a narrow spray angle and using the paint fairly dry. Flatting, stopping and finally applying the top coat follow as before.

Doors, bonnet and bootlid are all tackled the same way, but off the car. It's assumed that you already tried them up for correct fitting before beginning the re-spray!

Our Midget, painted and being fitted-up with ancilliary parts.

as well as heat (as do paraffin stoves).

When you have finished spraying, a fan heater can be used to assist the paint hardening off. Professionals use a bank of heat/light units, and you could build yourself a rack of these; they're also very useful as general garage lighting, especially in the winter! Dust, surprisingly, is not a great problem in home conditions; just avoid disturbing any on the floor and walls for some hours before spraying, but if there's lots on the floor, it can be layed by sprinkling with water, as shown in our heading picture. You're bound to get a few specks landing on the paint before it's totally dried, but these usually polish out when you undertake the last stage of all, the cutting and polishing of the final colour coats.

Well, this feature isn't intended to be a blow-by-blow account of how to spray your car, but more to point out the particular problems you face re-spraying at home. And take our word for it — superb results *can* be obtained by the dedicated amateur with next to no equipment in an ordinary-sized single garage. It just takes time. □

Spridget Rebuild/16

Coincidentally, two of our major rebuilds are at roughly the same stage — that of fitting-up after a major body rebuild and repaint. So some of my opening remarks in the VW instalment about this point in a rebuild are equally applicable to the 1275 Midget, which is also receiving all its chrome and trim prior to the rebuilt engine being installed.

Before this actually got properly underway though, a few last-minute tweaks were needed in the bodywork department; the scope for adjusting the bonnet fit wasn't enough so the standard procedure of carefully levering the hinges was resorted to so that the best fit was obtained, while similar controlled brutality was applied to a door which stuck out — this was pushed in at the bottom to twist it into the right shape. Additionally, and this was rather dodgier and not necessarily quite such good practice(!), the bottom of the door was also tapped inwards very gently, this being needed because ignoring our own advice, the rubber door seals hadn't been installed during the bare-metal trial fit of the doors. These can often make a difference and shuld always be put on when final adjustments are being made to the door fit before painting.

Then there was a bit of additional work centering around the radiator grille, or rather the chrome trim which surrounds it and mounts in the air intake. It was pop-rivetted into place but some quite skilled panel beating was required on the curvature of the front wings at this point to enable them to fit, due to the wings (which were 'pattern' parts) not being quite the right shape. Most holes needed for trim strips and other chrome attachments had been drilled prior to the bodyshell being painted incidentally; this minimises damage to the new paint, and ensures that no unpainted metal exists where rust could set in, as could happen if holes were drilled after painting.

Talking of rust, the bodyshell was thoroughly Waxoyled before any trim went in. This was simply a matter of ensuring that

all box sections and seams were treated; holes were drilled only when really necessary, and it was found that access to most places already existed — for instance you can get into the sills from the inner sills, the floor cross-member you can treat from under the seats, and from the jacking points. Only a few holes needed drilling, mainly in the boot area, and these were grommeted afterwards. The underside had already been sealed.

When it comes to bolting back all the ancillary bits, a good deal of prior preparation is necessary. Not only should you strip and refinish painted items, but you should also examine all captive nuts on these and on the car and run a thread cleaning tap through them — they're bound to be clogged up with old paint or under-sealant, or maybe new

paint. Then while you might want to renew all nuts and bolts (90% on our Spridget are new), there are always some special bolts or studs that have to be used again, and these should be carefully cleaned too, using a wire brush. It all adds up to hassle-free fitting up, and reduces the danger of crossed or stripped threads. Take a look at new components too — sometimes (as happened with our new radiator) they may come with holes not tapped.

One amusing point that emerged during the work concerned the window winder mechanism on one door — the end of the arm is cranked to give clearance when the glass is fully down, the cranking and shape stamped out by machine at the factory. But it had been noticed on this door that when wound three-

---

Exterior trim and fittings go on this month as the Midget races with the VW cabrio to get its engine in first!
More from Paul Skilleter.

Spridget Rebuild

This sort of tweaking may be necessary to finally achieve the correct fit, in this case with the bonnet.

Doors can be 'massaged' too; a wedge placed at the top will allow the door to be pushed inwards under pressure at the bottom, where it is lying proud of the body.

Here the holes are being drilled for the pop-rivets which will secure the grille surrounds; re-shaping of the insides of the wings was needed here to enable them to fit properly.

A home-made thread cleaning tap being made, by sawing a bolt. Cleaning-up threads is an important precautionary measure before reassembling components onto the shell.

Fitting trim to top of door; special bolts slide into the trim and these must line up with holes in top of door. You don't need a bolt in every hole though — four or five is ample.

This is the heater after dismantling, cleaning, flushing (of matrix) and painting. All joints were packed with rubber foam to prevent air leaks and rattles.

A Holts aerosol was used for refinishing minor components (like this petrol filler pipe), more convenient than keeping a full-size spraygun primed and clean.

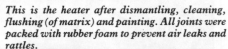

Fuel tank was checked, cleaned and repainted; also check sender unit is working (and is the right type — our first one turned out to be an MGB and didn't fit!), and remember to wire it up prior to refitting tank — you can't get at it afterwards.

Wiring loom was laid in car; here the wiper circuit is being checked by multi-meter. If old wires are snipped off components, tags left on show what wires and colours go where when you fit the new loom.

CONTINUED ON PAGE 77

Spridget Rebuild/17

This is being written just before Christmas and because all the pictures illustrating the Midget's interior trim fitting are stuck in the post, we can't round-off that part of the rebuild in this issue as intended. But at least the car itself is all complete and ready for trailering to our Beckenham centre of operations (from Lindsay Porter's workshop) for the rebuilt 1275 engine to be installed.

Meanwhile we can show a few items not mentioned previously, and can promise that we'll be covering the fitting-out of the car's interior next month instead. The car itself should be running by about the time you read

The grille surround has been a job to fit because the inner curvature of the replacement wings were not spot-on – but having corrected that, the whole grille could be offered up.

The rebuilt and repainted heater assembly is mounted on the bulkhead; new air ducting was installed afterwards.

Checking the position of the inertia-reel seatbelts these are strictly speaking non-original, but as we anticipated actively using the Midget, we thought this concession to convenience was forgiveable.

We did however, take the trouble to locate and fit the correct type of inner door handle – there are two types but the black plastic one is correct for the sort of door fitted to our car.

this too; and if not next issue, or certainly the one after, we'll be able to assess how successful the rebuild has been from the driving point of view.

Finally, Spridgebits (who've supplied nearly all the parts used during the project) have sent us their new, revised catalogue. This highly-detailed 84-page publication is a valuable guide to Spridgets in itself, whether you actually buy anything or not, and also contains various technical hints and tips on the cars, besides a new 3-page section on the maintenance, inspection and overhaul of the front suspension. Well worth getting – and it comes for the price of a 30p stamp! □

Chassis work has completed with a diff. change, which meant removing the half shaft.

Diff. assembly could then be lifted up into place on the axle.

An interim report as the GPO halts progress!

Spridget Rebuild/18

One of the best things about even post-Frogeye Sprites and Midgets is that almost monthly, more and more items become available from the specialists, easily keeping pace with deletions from the official BL range; indeed, you can now get some parts which haven't been offered by official dealers for years — trim parts being typical of these.

For instance, Spridgebits' new catalogue (issue 11, October 1984) lists eighteen different full carpet sets covering all models and colours from 1958 until 1980, rebuilt seats on exchange (at about £50 each), seat cover kits (around £35 each), and complete trim panel sets in colours to match whatever seats you have — these include door panels (casings), inner sill, inner footwell, front and rear bulkhead and rear wheel arch panels, and range from about £40 for the simple Frogeye of 1958-1961 to £68.50 for the more complex post-1969 cars. Or, you can buy all the individual trim panels separately.

Heater air duct needs a filter so you don't get an inrush of dead flies and leaves clogging things up; if you can't find a new one, make one like we did out of a piece of mesh.

Corrugated air trunking being fitted; this is obtainable new for under £6 and as it shows, is a worthwhile investment.

Inserting the door glass seal to inside of door — they're clipped to top of door frame by 'W' shaped clips; a special tool is required for this job — a piece of bent brazing rod . . .

Completing the re-trim — and we're nearly ready for the road! News of our 1969 Midget restoration from Paul Skilleter and Lindsay Porter.

Here the door capping rail has been installed, and the apertures in the frame are being sealed; you can use glue or mastic to stick the plastic in place, but it's important to do the job properly otherwise water will ruin the trim panels.

On this 1969 Midget, the centre trim panel is steel-backed and has to be pop-rivetted to the door frame.

The new outer trim panel could then be offered up, tucking up under capping rail.

Door latch surround and latch goes on . . .

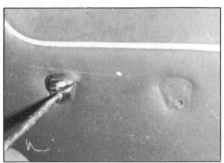

. . . followed by grab handle, one bracket for this being screwed in position, the handle itself inserted in both brackets, then the 'loose' bracket screwed into place.

Window winder is screwed to its mechanism; check angle of winder so that with window closed it lays at a convenient angle. Our car has the correct 'easi-break'(!) type plastic handles.

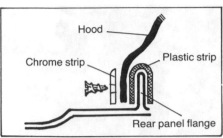

This diagram shows in cross-section how the hood is secured across the rear cockpit flange.

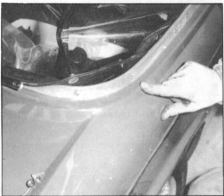

Orthodox press-stud clips are fitted to body sides where hood is detachable; matching ones are already in place on BL replacement hood.

Hood fitting: the rear of the hood is permanently fitted to the rear cockpit surround by screws and a chrome strip, and include studs to accept the tonneau cover.

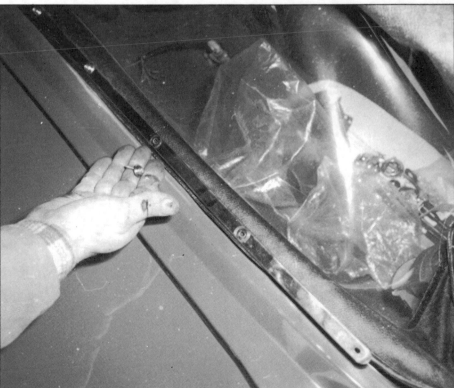

Velcro strips also come on side flaps of the BL hood, but you need to attach strips of the same material to body sides.

The very cold weather made it impossible for the hood to be closed, and heat had to be conducted to the plastic to allow it to stretch and close!

After you've checked the relative positions, the press-studs are screwed into the floor to take the carpets.

The carpets are then fitted down; side and rear trim panels, all of which can now be purchased new, have also been installed.

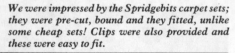

We were impressed by the Spridgebits carpet sets; they were pre-cut, bound and they fitted, unlike some cheap sets! Clips were also provided and these were easy to fit.

The neatly-made transmission tunnel carpeting — the trickiest bit to make if you're cutting your own carpet — slots over the gear lever turret. Rubber gaiter for gear lever is obtainable new.

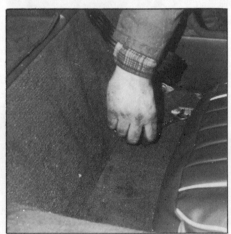

One of the last jobs was to bolt the seat-runners down, sliding seat forward to reach the rear bolts, then back to get at the front; check for easy running of seat before finally tightening bolts — you may need to alter the angle of the runners slightly.

For our car, being red, we chose a correct red/white piping trim and very smart it looks too. Fitting the new parts was not difficult, though it pays to offer all the items up first to check. We started with the doors first, then the various internal trim panels, then the carpets and finally the seats. The hood was an authentic BL item, and was of very good quality. Yes, we're almost there — just the engine and box to go back in now! □

NEXT MONTH
1275cc engine rebuild.

Spridget Rebuild/19

The engine from our Midget has been transferred to Eric Gilbert's workshop at Beckenham for its overhaul, all part of our plan to occupy Eric for 24 hours of each day. Eric's first job was to remove the worst of the oil and dirt from the exterior of the engine, this being well worth doing and relatively easy at this stage.

Dismantling the engine was straightfor-

Our usual procedure applied prior to the strip-down: Firstly Eric cleaned the worst of the oily dirt from the outside of the engine, and made available a selection of containers into which to put related parts as they were removed from the engine. Ancilliary components such as the carburettors were removed from the engine but not dismantled at this stage.

ward enough and I do not propose to cover it in detail. The ancilliaries were removed first to get them out of the way, followed by the carburettors and manifolds. The exhaust manifold was found to be broken adjacent to number four exhaust port.

The removal of the rocker cover revealed an almost dry carbon coating on the rockers and valve gear. The rocker shaft appeared to be in good condition. This was removed and put to one side for cleaning and closer examination. It is worth mentioning at this stage

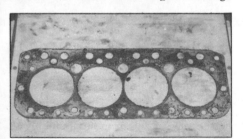

A blackened gasket as can be seen here between Nos 2 and 3 cylinders indicates that there had been a gas leak — there is also evidence of water leaks.

that a collection of boxes or other suitable receptacles is useful for storing various parts as they are removed from the engine. Keeping components together in groups in this way helps to ensure that nothing is lost and nothing forgotten during reassembly.

Next the cylinder head was removed and we found that there had been water leaks into some cylinders and that the tops of some pistons had been damaged — quite severely pitted in fact — by water in the cylinders. There was evidence of a gas and water leak between

As our Spridget project nears completion John Williams describes the engine overhaul.

Spridget Rebuild

We hope to produce a Midget of slightly enhanced performance, and will be fitting this reconditioned head (from Spridgebits) which has been gas flowed and ported.

This flywheel ring gear can be seen to be thoroughly worn and we have since fitted a new ring gear.

Number 2 piston (the second from right) is badly pitted due to the presence of water in the cylinder. Number four cylinder was chipped due to loose solid matter in the cylinder.

The internals of this engine were in an unusually dirty condition. We were not surprised to discover that the crankshaft will have to be ground.

numbers two and three cylinders, and the absence of green paint from part of the exterior of the engine suggested that water

was escaping past the head gasket and down the side of the engine.

The pistons were removed and the piston

rings were heavily carboned, indeed the top ring on numper one piston was siezed tightly into the piston groove. It would be interesting to know when this engine was last in use and how it ran. Eric Gilbert expressed the view that the engine had had little use with long periods of rest in between, and in addition to burning a large amount of oil — and it became clear that dirty oil had remained in use for a long time — it bore a closer resemblance to a steam engine than an internal combustion engine.

The bearings all displayed a mottled grey colour due to pitting, and the crankshaft journals were discoloured in patches on the thrust side.

The clutch was corroded but far from worn, but there was a great deal of wear on the flywheel ring gear.

To summarise, the exhaust manifold would have to be replaced. The cylinder block will have to be skimmed (a new head will be fitted anyway), and it will require a rebore (and new pistons), plus the crankshaft will need to be ground. □

NEXT MONTH
Rebuilding the engine.

CONTINUED FROM PAGE 23
was fitted here, rebated to obtain a flush-fit — and if you haven't a 'joddler', this effect can be achieved using just a hammer and cold chisel.

What you do is to establish where you want the step to begin and mark the spot, place the piece of steel in the vice, and cold chisel it back. This invariably bends the top part of

The new repair section is now finished and can be welded to the shut-pillar.

the metal back, so bring it up straight again using hammer and dolly. Hit the crease again with the chisel, bring it back straight again as before, repeat the operation another two or three times and you will end up with a nice little step which will allow you to fit the new repair panel with its main surface flush with the existing panel. Try it for yourself! □

NEXT MONTH
Rear wheel arch repairs, including fabricating your own repair sections.

Spridget Rebuild/20

The reassembly of our 1275cc Midget engine started with refitting the bearings to the crankcase, the crankshaft itself (which has been ground 10 thou undersize and has bearings to suit), and the thrust washers which fit on either side of the crank centre journal with their grooves facing away from the journal. Plenty of oil should be applied to all the bearings and the thrust washers during reassembly. The flywheel is fitted (temporarily) to the crankshaft so that the tightness of the crankshaft can be felt as it is being torqued down. The final torque setting for the bolts which secure the main bearing caps should be 60lbs/ft and this is reached in easy stages, turning the crankshaft to check that although it may be quite tight it does not seize up completely.

The next job is to fit the pistons noting that the numbers on the connecting rods face the camshaft side of the engine. The pistons for our engine are new, and the connecting rods have been heated in order to insert the gud-

We started at the bottom of the engine. The bearing shells are in place here. Note the lubrication holes in the bearings which align with oil galleries in the block.

geon pins which are now a tight fit in the rods but floating in the pistons. The big end bolts are ⅜″ bolts which, according to the manual, should be tightened to 40lbs/ft.

Next we replaced the front engine plate and gasket, the eight camshaft followers, the camshaft and the camshaft thrust plate. The latter can only be fitted one way as indicated by the position of the three screws. The camshaft thrust bearing end float should be checked and this should be between 0.0045″

and 0.085″ (0.12-0.21mm). We fitted the oil pick-up making sure that the gland nut was tight in the block, and then the sump. The main bearing cap seals are purchased as straight lengths of cork which have to be soaked for some time in engine oil in order to allow them to expand and become pliable. When fitted, these seals are trimmed so that about ⅛″ is left protruding, and this surplus will be compressed as the sump is tightened to create a good seal. Where the ends of the

Reassembling the engine, John Williams reports

Spridget Rebuild

Torqueing up the crankshaft bolts in the correct order and in easy stages using the flywheel to turn the shaft so as to feel for any sudden tightness.

The pistons were fitted using a clamp to compress the rings and (though it cannot be seen here) plenty of engine oil.

The engine plate is attached to the block by means of these two screws (using an Allen key) on which Eric used a dab of Locktite, rather than locking washers which could break as the screws are countersunk. These screws are fitted BEFORE the camshaft sprocket.

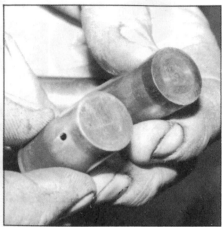

Old and new cam followers: the old one has the oil hole which is visible here.

The crankshaft and camshaft sprockets must be carefully aligned by means of shims behind the crankshaft sprocket. When the number of shims has been decided the sprockets can be taken off the engine and fitted with the chain.

sump gasket meet their cork seals we used Blue Hylomar gasket sealant (though similar products by Holts, Comma, etc could be used instead) to ensure an oil tight seal.

Next we trial fitted the camshaft and crankshaft sprockets using enough shims behind the crankshaft sprocket to ensure that both sprockets were level with each other. Then the sprockets were removed and refitted, but this time complete with the Duplex chain and the timing marks aligned (see picture). The oil thrower goes onto the crankshaft after the sprocket (note that it is marked 'F' for forward, to ensure that it is fit-

The sprockets should be placed in the chain so that the two timing marks, arrowed here, lie close together on the line between the centres of the sprockets. The whole assembly is then lifted into place on the engine.

Although the timing marks have moved apart in this picture the timing is still correct as the sprockets have not been allowed to jump out of the chain. When using old locking washers fold a new part of the washer each time it is re-used. Re-using old folds can lead to breakages.

ted the right way around), followed by the timing case cover complete with the crankshaft front oil seal which should be well greased to provide initial lubrication, followed by the pulley and then the lock washer and nut.

Our Duplex chain has a link and spring clip (some are continuous chains) and as I have indicated already these should be fitted before the chain, complete with sprockets, is offered up to the engine as an assembly. The link should pass through the chain from the engine side, and the clip should be fitted in such a way that its open end faces away from the direction of the chain's movement.

The timing case cover should not be bolted up firmly until the crankshaft pulley has been fitted and revolved a few times to centralise the cover, and thus avoiding any distortion of the oil seal which would rapidly lead to failure of the seal. The bolts which secure the cover are of different lengths, the longest ones passing into the cylinder block itself.

It is worth turning the engine over from time to time to make sure that there is

The oil seal (in the right hand aperture in the timing case as seen here) is fitted before the timing case cover is attached to the engine and should be well greased to provide the initial lubrication. The oil thrower is now in place, hiding the camshaft sprocket in this picture.

nothing locking up as components are added. Better to discover such problems sooner rather than later.

The oil pump and its cover is fitted next after priming it with clean engine oil, ensuring that it is the right way up by placing the indentation on the pump uppermost. Next the rear engine plate was fitted followed by the flywheel, remembering the locking ring for the six flywheel bolts, the torque setting for the latter being 40lbs/ft. Eric Gilbert greased the spigot bearing (in the centre of the flywheel) and fitted the clutch assembly at this stage.

We obtained a replacement cylinder head from Spridgbits. This was a reconditioned head which had been gas flowed, and it came complete with valves and springs. We fitted the pushrods, and rocker shaft components from the old head, and also transferred all the necessary studs for the manifolds, thermostat housing etc.

The water pump and fan were also fitted

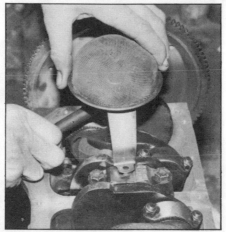

The oil pick-up assembly should be fitted very firmly to the block so that there is no risk of air leaks interfering with oil circulation.

Our cylinder head came complete with valves and springs. Had it not done so we would have needed a valve spring compressor but otherwise the reassembly of the rocker shaft, rockers etc., is straightforward. Note the old sparking plugs which are in place to prevent debris from getting into the cylinders. It is also worth noting that it is a good idea to clean the threads on the studs which go into the block and the head as damaged or dirty threads will interfere with torque readings.

and the next task will be refitting the engine in the car and looking at other ancillaries. □

Next Month
Refitting the engine and attention to the ancillaries.

Spridget Rebuild/21

Our MkIII MG Midget is now almost ready to go on the road. We expect it to be at our Bromley Pageant of Motoring on June 16th, and since the car will be looking for a new home by then it may well be at Bromley that it will meet its next owner!

The starter motor

The starter motor was very dirty externally and we dismantled it to check whether the brushes were badly worn, the armature clean and its grooves clear, and the internal wiring sound. Before dismantling the motor the Bendix gear can be examined for wear or actual damage, and a check can be carried out to see whether there is excessive end play affecting the shaft running through the motor, or lateral movement which indicates

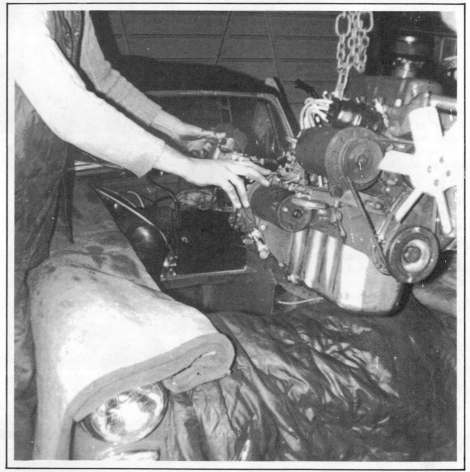

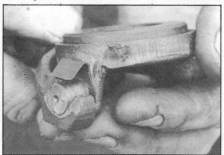

A small detail but it must be correct – the clips which attach the clutch bearing mounting to the operating arm slip over the lugs on each side of the mounting which is then placed in the fork of the arm...

...then both clips are inverted as shown here.

bearing wear.

Two long bolts are removed to release the end cover from the motor, but it should not be pulled off immediately. The inside of the cover carries four brush assemblies, two of which are connected to the motor's windings. By removing the dust cover around the main casing you can gain access to these brushes and release them from their holders so that the end cover can be removed. Then, allowing these two brushes to remain attached to the windings, the main casing can also be lifted away.

Once cleaned, our starter motor proved to be in a fairly good condition, so we reassembled it with a little grease on the bearings at both ends (removing excess grease to that it would not spread to the electrical parts) and remembering to check the condition of the main feed terminal insulator. Had it been necessary as we could have reduced end play by adding a clean, lightly greased, washer to the shaft inside the end cover.

When refitting the starter motor to the engine it is worth ensuring that the dust cover

Overhauling ancillaries and installing the engine. by John Williams

After the small central mounting (A) has been loosely attached to the bottom of the gearbox extension, the main mounting assembly (B) is attached too, all bolts being tightened evenly to ensure satisfactory alignment.

Dismantling the starter motor: Start by removing the dust cover to give access to the four brush assemblies. Two brushes are connected to the windings in the motor and have to be withdrawn (use bent wire to control the springs and pointed pliers to withdraw the brushes) to allow removal of end plates.

screw is accessible, and that the battery lead is positioned as far as possible from any component which can be expected to become hot.

The dynamo

We started by cleaning the exterior and checking for end play (same remedy as for the starter motor), and then removed the pulley and fan. Then we removed the end plate from the opposite end of the dynamo and this comes away complete with two brush assemblies. The outer casing can then be removed. The internals of our dynamo

The end plate removed – the brushes were not badly worn as the ones still attached to the motor on the left demonstrate.

The commutator grooves should be square in section (not V shaped) so clean them with care.

Very lightly grease the bearings at both ends of the starter motor. If end play is such that reducing it as suggested in the text causes commutator to be off centre in relation to the brushes, you will have to dismantle the Bendix gear etc to add further shims or a thin washer where the existing shim is shown (arrowed) here.

needed a thorough clean for which we used petrol and allowed it plenty of time to dry. We took care to keep the petrol away from the bearing in the pulley end of the dynamo so as to avoid diluting the pre-packed lubrication in that bearing. The commutator (against which the brushes run) was black, but a bright finish was reinstated using very fine glasspaper, and its grooves were cleaned out.

The brushes were well worn with cracked insulation on their wires and corroded screws

– these were renewed. A thin smear of grease was applied to the end cover bearing (brushes end) and the windings were given a light spray of WD40 to protect against damp. Don't forget to replace any shims or spacer washers which were present before refitting the end cover.

If it necessary to strike the spindle to loosen the dynamo pulley, do so lightly and only with the nut in place to protect the threads.

With dynamo pulley and fan removed (the Woodruffe key on which they locate is arrowed) the 'works' can be removed from casing for cleaning and inspection. Throughout any jobs on electrical components watch out for broken wires, perished or cracked insulation etc.

The carburettors

Our Midget is is fitted with twin 1¼″ SU carburettors. The important check on these is for wear in the butterfly spindles and their housings in the carburettor body. Spindles can be replaced but if the carburettor body is badly worn where a spindle passes through you might as well look for new or better carburettors. The alternative is to have the body bored out and bushed to fit a new spindle – a precision job which will not be cheap.

We dismantled the carburettors for cleaning and this was badly needed. The suction chamber is secured by screws around its perimeter and comes away with the piston, damper and needle assembly. The float chamber can be unscrewed from the side of the carburettor after the petrol feed pipe has

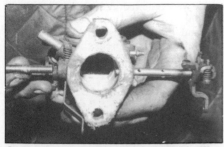

Carburettor spindle wear is usually visible. Wear in the housing is sometimes visible too and can certainly be detected by using a new or unworn spindle. Alternatively, housing wear can be checked using a clean drill shank of the same diameter as an unworn section of the existing spindle.

been disconnected from the bottom of the chamber, then the lid of the chamber can be unscrewed so that the needle valve and float can be removed and inspected and the chamber itself cleaned out. Finally, the choke linkage should be disconnected from the base of the carburettor and the jet block unscrewed.

We fitted new spindles and new needle valves but otherwise all that our carburettors needed was a good clean.

Re-assembly of the carburettors really is dismantling in reverse; *but*, the jet locking nut should not be tightened at first but left slack until the choke linkage is reconnected, and until you are satisfied that the needle is centralised – that is, the piston and needle assembly should be capable of rising and falling over its full range of movement without sticking. You check this by pushing the piston up

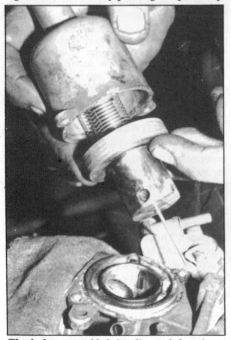

The dashpot assembly being dismantled – primarily for cleaning.

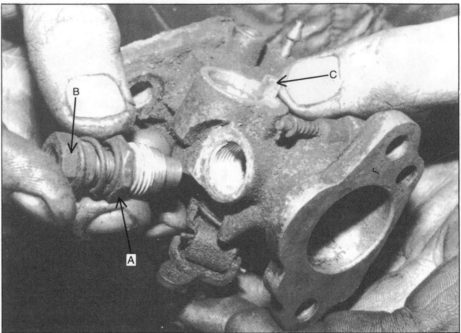

The jet block is removed from the base of the carburettor by disconnecting the linkage then unscrewing the locking and centralising nut (A). Spring loaded nut (B) is the mixture control. Note also the small tab (C) which ensures that the float chamber is correctly located.

into the suction chamber with a screwdriver or similar (taking care not to damage the piston) and allowing it and the needle to fall of its own accord. You should keep checking this whilst tightening the jet locking nut. Then screw up the adjusting nut to its fullest extent still checking that the piston/needle assembly rises and falls freely. Then unscrew the adjusting nut about 11 'flat's' – this is a good starting point for final tuning.

Refitting the engine

This was definitely a two-man job, one to operate the hoist whilst the other manipulated the engine. The engine and gearbox were reunited away from the car and then lifted, so that they remained level, by the hoist. We then tilted the assembly by hand as the hoist lowered it into the engine bay. In retrospect it might have been easier had we attached the assembly to the hoist in such a way that the gearbox tilted downwards about 30 degrees in the first place, but our method worked.

The offside engine mounting and bracket were fitted to the body, but on the nearside we fitted the mounting/bracket assembly to the engine itself. The radiator was still out of the car at this stage but even so there was not much room to spare as the gearbox was juggled into the transmission tunnel. The engine/gearbox assembly had to be tilted steeply to clear the front panel yet still enter the tunnel but it did not take long to align it with the offside engine mounting after which the nearside engine mounting bracket seemed to find its bolt holes in the body almost automatically.

Finally (for this month anyway) a big

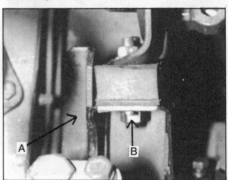

The nearside front engine mounting and bracket correctly fitted. The brackets are marked R (right) and L (left) if the paper labels are still intact and legible but can still be fitted incorrectly. The reinforcing piece (A) should be on the radiator side of the bracket, and the small stud through the back of the mounting is above the securing nut (B) when fitted.

'Thank You' to Spridgebits Ltd of Birmingham (tel: 021-554 2033), and the Sprite and Midget Centre of Richmond (tel: 01-984 6464), who have supplied parts to our Worcester and Beckenham workshops respectively and whose expert advice has been a vital ingredient of this rebuild. □

Next month
Finishing touches and road testing.

Spridget Finished!

It all began in our October 1983 issue — a very tired Midget indeed was displayed on our cover, coloured green and looking very sorry for itself. About the only points in its favour were that it could just about motor under its own steam (which helped us assess what wanted doing mechanically), and had not been messed about with too much. In short, it was the type of car decribed in for-sale ads as 'ideal for restoration' — which, of course, was the whole purpose of buying the car in the first place.

The following twenty instalments duly chronicled all that happened to the Midget during that rebuild, beginning with the engine and gearbox removal, through all the bodywork restoration (which included inner and outer sills, floorpans, hinge pillars, inner rear wings, rear spring mountings and rear

How our Midget arrived, lines of rust bubbles in the hinge pillars, sills and rear wings hinting at the corrosion under the dull green paintwork.

bulkhead, front inner wings, front panel, front chassis rails, front outer wings and rear wing sections — all these being replaced or repaired), front suspension rebuild, rear axle check and ending with a home respray in Tartan red cellulose.

As we've said before, one of the pleasant aspects of restoring a Spridget these days is

the marvellous range of parts available. Ours were almost all supplied by Spridgebits, who provided an excellent service especially when it came to searching out the unusual or obscure — as their customers have reason to be grateful for, Spridgebits differ from some other MG specialists in continuing to supply second-hand parts, from the numerous examples they're broken over the years. So our thanks to Graham Sykes and Jed Watts for a great parts back up.

Then Lindsay Porter it was who masterminded the body and chassis rebuild; faced with an extremely rusty car, he made sure that it was turned into one of the nicest Midgets we've seen, and we'd particularly like to thank Ken Wright, who continues to apply his skills though now for Autoprep of Martley, Lindsay having discontinued his restoration activities in favour of writing more books on the subject.

Eric Gilbert rebuilt the 1275cc engine, and

Our MG Midget returns to the road —
Paul Skilleter reviews its rebuild and tries it out.

Spridget Finished!

As the paint was stripped so the rust became more evident; lights and chrome were removed and checked for replacement or replating.

when it was fired up for the first time a few weeks ago in June, it was as expected a faultless runner. We certainly savoured that first run in the car — my own impressions are that it really did feel like a 'new' Midget, one that had just come off the production line. Obviously we were keeping engine revs down but the little power unit pulled smoothly and sweetly, the gearbox is excellent (it wasn't touched bar a couple of oil seals, about the only major item not needing attention during the restoration!), and the steering was very precise. A brief 'PDI' revealed only a non-functional rev. counter and a slight clonk from somewhere at the back, plus the reinstatement of the horn operation to the steering wheel centre — Eric had to rig up a temporary switch pending the arrival of the missing parts from the Sprite and Midget

The end result — note the correct grille, not the MGB one seen offered up in one 'interim' episode which caused much derision at the time but, in the rush to get to press, no-one noticed (or can now explain why it was shown with the car at all!).

Here the outer sills and lower part of the rear wing has been cut away, revealing the rot in the underlying bodywork. Lindsay holds a new inner sill panel . . .

. . . which is seen in place here with the outer sill being tried up.

Nice thing about a Spridget is that it's light enough to be manhandled upside down, which makes welding and refinishing the underside very convenient.

Centre, Richmond (who have also been most helpful following the arrival of the Midget at Beckenham after its rebuild in the Midlands).

The only unsatisfactory aspect of the car is

Spridgebits were able to supply all new chrome and the wire wheels were new too. Only the quarterlight frames haven't been changed.

A reconditioned crackle-black instrument panel was installed, and of the detail work remaining, the dash lighting is playing up, a new horn push mechanism is required, and the rev. counter (working when we drove the unrestored car) has to be persuaded to function.

that it's too good for us to use as a staff car, and we've reluctantly decided to sell it. It seemed silly to turn it back into a high-mileage used car once again after all the work that's been put into it, and we thought it

The rebuilt engine in its bay; air cleaners are non-original but the factory-type proved temporarily elusive.

Ready for action; our Midget has only a dozen or so miles on the clock at the moment, but given the right weather, running it in should be an enjoyable experience.

would be more appropriate to leave KWL 499G as enthusiast transport. After all, something like £3,000-worth (retail) of parts have gone into our Midget, with at least that much again in labour, so it's hardly material for a staff hack!

Meanwhile we shall continue to run it in, getting maybe a few hundred miles on the clock to make sure everything is working as it should. In that way we'll be able to enjoy the fruits of everyone's efforts for a little while at least, and also the sheer fun motoring that these little sports cars provide. We just hope that the rest of the summer provides in turn the sort of weather which the car deserves! □

CONTINUED FROM PAGE 62

Rustproofing was a vital step taken at this time: here the rear wheel-arches are being treated.

Access to cross-members and sills can be found via the jacking points. A de Vilbiss wax injector is being used here, but the hand-operated gear is also affective if slower.

Not too much drilling was required, but collar was used over bit to prevent drill from hitting the other side of a cavity — which if an outer panel could be a disaster!

Bumper irons had to be re-shaped and painted; here they've been replaced and are being checked with a straight-edge to ensure they're level.

Offering up the bumper can be very difficult without scratching the paint, so protecting ends of bumper with rags would be a good precaution, though there's not much clearance with the wings.

quarters down, you felt a click and nothing more happened. On examination it turned out that the arm was cranked the wrong way, the only explanation for this being that the part must have been fed into the machine upside down. Yet the original owner of the car obviously had never complained about it when the car was new! □

NEXT MONTH
Retrimming the interior.

Sprites & Midgets

*Cheap to buy,
inexpensive to run
and fun to drive —
Michael Brisby says that the
Sprites and Midgets still have a lot to offer.*

The more you think about MG Midgets and Austin Healey Sprites the more there is to admire about them. Forget for a moment that the cars are neither rare or exotic — for eighteen years various versions of the same basic recipe provided a great many people with a lot of low-cost open air motoring fun and I would highly recommend the cars to anyone looking for just those qualities.

If a group of engineers sat down today and set out to design an open car which was small, economical to make and run, well mannered and used well-tried mechanical components they might well come up with a car not at all unlike the Sprite and Midget family. The unfortunate thing is that the Sprite departed in 1971 and by the time the Midget died in 1979

it had had one heart transplant too many and it was none too steady on its feet — the chances of a worthy successor being born look pretty thin since the marketing men have convinced themselves that simple open sportscars will not sell.

As we suggested in a recent *Practical Classics* editorial there is now no basic, for-the-fun-of-it, open sports car selling at a rock bottom price on the British market and I suspect that there are going to be plenty of people looking for Sprites and Midgets over the next few years, some who cannot find a modern alternative, and those who see the car as worth preserving in its own right.

The Background

The Donald Healey Motor Company took a few bits from the staid BMC range including some unwanted Austin Atlantic engines that were surplus to requirements and conjured up the

Healey 100 — Leonard Lord of BMC saw the car, put aside his personal disinterest in sports cars, and quickly formulated an agreement for the car to be marketed through the BMC dealerships as an *Austin* Healey.

The relationship proved a success and went a step further when both men saw the market for a smaller sports car, again using BMC mechanical components as a basis and with the proviso that the car must be cheap to build. The result was the chirpy Austin Healey Sprite which appeared in 1958 and quickly earned the affectionate 'Frog Eye' title on account of the headlamps protruding from the one piece

Cheap to build, cheap and enjoyable to run, the Austin Healey Sprite appeared in 1958 and has been popular ever since. A "Frog Eye" in good condition with a steel bonnet is very much in demand as reflected by the prices they can fetch, but restorable examples can still offer good value.

Sprites & Midgets

In 1961 the Sprite was re-skinned losing its curves and becoming more angular. It gained a boot lid in the process and the Midget was born. In 1964 wind-up windows and external door locks were accompanied by a better hood and the rear suspension was changed. This is a 1,098 c.c. Midget which is showing its age.

bonnet and wing assembly. Originally it was intended that the lamps would retract when not in use but this was considered too expensive and the resultant compromise did a great deal to make the car instantly recognisable.

Individual appearance was only part of the success of the Sprite, as it would never have made the grade if it had not been what it set out to be — a cheap, agile, economical and reliable little sports car that was enormous fun to drive and capable of accepting alarming degrees of modification without complaint.

To broaden the appeal of the Sprite it was given what amounted to a new outer skin in 1961 — to put it crudely the car lost its resemblance to a used bar of soap, with protruding headlamps to denote the front end, becoming instead almost brick-like. The one-piece bonnet and wing assembly was replaced by fixed wings and a separate bonnet and the rear of the car was given a boot lid (the original Sprite boot space could only be loaded from the rear of the cockpit). In some ways the new outward appearance was a foretaste of the yet to be announced MGB, and in a deliberate ploy

to trade on MG loyalties an MG Midget version of the Sprite was invented by providing changes to the front grille, badges and trim and offering the result at a higher price than the Sprite.

Both cars retained the Frog Eye, or Mk I Sprite, 948c.c. A-series engine and rear suspension incorporating trailing quarter-elliptic leaf springs with axle location assisted by radius arms.

In the Autumn of 1962 both the Sprite and Midget were given a 1098c.c. engine increasing power output by 5 b.h.p. to 55 b.h.p. Contemporary road test results indicate that maximum speed with the bigger engine was only up by 2 m.p.h. but the cars now had disc brakes in place of drums at the front.

A major change in 1964 saw the replacement of the quarter-elliptic springs on the rear suspension by semi-elliptics. To make the cars more habitable the sidescreens were discarded and the new doors to incorporate wind-up windows were provided with external door handles. To round off the improvements both cars were given a considerably better hood and benefitted from somewhat less-basic

seats and interior trim. The cars had become much more civilised and had a wider market appeal.

The attractions of both the Sprite and Midget were further enhanced in 1966 with the replacement of the 1,098c.c. engine by a 1,275c.c. version of the A-series unit. This was not the Mini-Cooper S engine, but it did make for what many people regard as the best version of the cars.

In 1971 the Austin Healey Sprite was discontinued and in 1974 the Midget was modified to meet American safety and emission regulations. The changes cannot be described as improvements. A 1,493c.c. engine (that from the Spitfire 1500 along with its gearbox in non-overdrive form) which met the American exhaust emission controls but offered only marginally more power was employed to drive a car which weighed 200 lbs more by the time 5 m.p.h. impact resistant "plastic" bumpers and other safety devices had been added to the car.

The worse aspect of these changes was a one inch increase in ride height which noticeably harmed the car's handling capabilities — the chief attraction of the Sprite and Midget range for many enthusiasts. During 1979 the Midget 1500 was phased out of production.

A well preserved Austin Sprite. Sprite production ceased in 1971 and some interest attaches to the point that the licence to build cars with Healey included in their title expired on the last day of 1970 — it appears that about 400 Austin Sprites were built.

THE ONES TO BUY

The Austin Healey Sprite in Frog Eye form has long been recognised as an old car worth having both by the classic car enthusiast and the general public. Its appeal is largely visual and performance with the 948c.c. engine is economical and fast enough to be fun while the handling, if the car is in good condition, is as responsive as any of the range.

The 948c.c. Mk II Sprite and Mk I Midget are generally treated as the poor relations of the family with the basic trim and power output of the Frog Eye without that car's individual appearance. However, if you don't *need* to have the looks of the Frog these cars represent quite a good bargain if you can find

The MG Midget at its best — with the 1,275 c.c. engine and before increased ride height and 5 m.p.h. bumpers to meet American safety legislation somewhat spoilt the car's appeal.

Sophisticated Sprites — John Sprinzel Racing built about 80 Sebring Sprites which were alloy bodied fixed head coupes with an entirely different screen arrangement and bonnet shape to the standard cars. Stirling and Pat Moss drove the cars at Sebring and Ian Walker, seen at Oulton Park in 1961, held the class lap record at every major British circuit that year.

a sound one — particularly an example with sound metal around the rear spring mountings. I rather suspect that many of the Mk II Sprites and Mk I Midgets have been neglected and that a high proportion of those that have survived may have had a bigger engine fitted.

The 1,098c.c. cars (they retained the same Mark numbers as the 948c.c. cars) are not notably faster than their earlier relations but they do have disc brakes at the front which may be desirable — I have generally found that the drum braked cars stopped quite adequately, however.

Considerably better weather protection of the Mk 3 Sprite and Mk 2 Midget make them a rather more attractive car for regular use than their immediate predecessors. These cars have semi-elliptic rear springs and the mountings were subjected to less strain but on very rusty cars the springs *can* poke through the floor. The 1,098c.c. engine stands up to normal usage quite well, but it is a long stroke unit and the smaller or later, larger engines are tougher.

The most popular Sprite or Midget after the Frog Eye is the 1,275c.c. version (Mk 4 Sprite, Mk 3 Midget) introduced in 1966. The interiors were civilised if not luxurious and the power unit well suited to the car, and I must admit that it is my favourite. The 1969-70 cars were treated to matt-black screen surrounds and sills and Rostyle wheels — both very period touches — but were otherwise unaltered.

Sprite production ceased in 1971, but the Midget survived until 1974 so there are a great many 1,275c.c. cars to choose from.

In 1974 the elevated, plastic wrapped and Triumph powered cars were let loose. In the eyes of most people with experience of the earlier cars these were a disappointment. It is

significant that the trade is not particularly fond of the engine and express reservations about its life expectancy. It remains to be seen whether the Midget 1500 eventually gains support amongst enthusiasts but it does have the major handicap of its inferior handling when compared to the earlier cars and therefore lacks one of the biggest attractions of the Sprites and Midgets.

The Lenham Le Mans Coupe gave the Sprites and Midgets an effective facelift — maximum speed benefitted too.

Specials

Since 129,354 Austin Healey Sprites and over 200,000 MG Midgets were made it stands to reason that special versions are in demand. Heading the list are the works competition cars — mainly Sprites — and the chances of finding a car that is not already accounted for are slim. If you do come across one, or a car that is claimed to be, you would be well advised to contact the appropriate club for confirmation.

More numerous and sharing the same degree of success were the Sebring Sprites

which were fixed head coupe bodies on the Sprite floorpan. These cars were accepted by the governing bodies of motor sport as production cars in their own right and about eighty were built by John Sprinzel Racing. A number of notable drivers including Pat and Stirling Moss and John Sprinzel himself drove the cars and the very fastest were capable of 120 m.p.h. with an engine capacity of less than a litre. As with the works cars it is a good idea to seek expert advice about the cars before buying and John Sprinzel is most approachable on the subject.

WSM Sprites and Midgets were similar to the Sebring in concept but with a more Ferrari 250GTO-like body. Opinions about how many were built vary — some people say two dozen and some suggest it was less. Very few survive.

Numerous firms made glass-fibre hardtops and bonnets for Sprites and Midgets including the Lenham Motor Company who went a stage further to produce a rather attractive body conversion comprising a one-piece bonnet and front wing assembly and a fixed head coupe moulding incorporating a new, abruptly cut-off, tail treatment. This conversion is still available and is claimed to improve maximum speed by 9 miles per hour due to improved air flow.

A number of tuning specialists saw a market for performance conversions to the Sprite and Midget range which had the handling to safely cope with rather more power and BMC Special Tuning, and their successors, could provide a pretty comprehensive range of performance parts. Superchargers were fitted by some enthusiasts but few cars have retained them in their old age.

Engine transplants were not uncommon at one time; Jack Brabham converted cars using a Coventry Climax overhead camshaft 1,216c.c. engine in place of the 948c.c. standard engine with predictably fast results and in the days of the 1275 cars the Atlantis Midget used a Ford 1600 GT engine and gearbox to give an MGB a very good run for its money.

WHAT TO LOOK FOR

It would be unfair to suggest that the Sprites and Midgets suffer from rust any more than other cars of a similar age, but while a sound

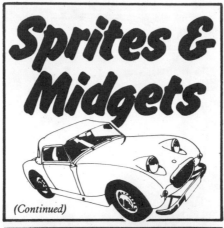

Sprites & Midgets

(Continued)

Two views that sum up how to judge the condition of a Midget or Sprite. External rust gives every indication that the sills are rotten. There is also plenty of evidence that the base of the front wing is full of road dirt and has rusted, the door pillar and lower areas of the rear wings also add to the evidence that this car needs a shell rebuild. This car has wind-up windows and water has got past the seals and attacked the door bottom. Do not buy a car like this unless you are prepared to spend time and money on it.

The joint between the sill and door-post or scuttle side should be clearly defined. The weld on this car is typical evidence of a rather basic repair — when this area rusts the bottom hinge breaks free.

shell is surprisingly strong considering its simple, light, construction, once rust gets a hold it quickly causes serious weakening of the structure.

There can be few cars where the sill structure is so vital and the rear suspension mountings run them a very close second in the order of priority checks you should make, before buying a Sprite of Midget.

At present there are enough cars about to allow would-be buyers to pick and choose and avoid cars in disastrous condition, and there is no reason (apart from insurance costs) why a young enthusiast should not be able to buy either a sound runnable car at a reasonable price or an easy restoration project for considerably less. The golden rule is not to buy rubbish and to pay less attention to the mechanical side (relatively easy to put right) and concentrate more on the body and trim the lower you go down the price range.

The first step when looking at the sills is to see whether the joints between the sills and the wings and front door post cum-scuttle side are as they should be — that is showing without any evidence of filler. The Frog Eye Sprite one-piece bonnet allows you to see the joint between the sill and bulkhead which is a trouble spot — on those cars with fixed front wings you will have to guess what lies behind.

The car may have had new sills fitted during its life and if so, make sure the welds are sound — lift the draught excluder at the door aperture and glance below the car to where the

On a Frog Eye Sprite you can lift the bonnet to inspect the sill top and condition of the front bulkhead side, on cars with fixed wings you may have to guess what lies behind. Removal of the wing on this car shows damage to the bulkhead and a quite incorrectly fitted replacement sill.

sill meets the floor pan and make sure the flanges are securely welded. With the door open you can exert a vice-like grip in the outer and inner sill and if anything gives or you hear rust flake falling inside the sill the car needs plenty of work.

While the door is open have a look at the bottom hinge mounting — as the car deteriorate the door post rusts away here. Close the door and check the door gap — if it is narrow across the top of the door this may be due to the sill being weakened by rust, frontal impact or by the car being allowed to warp during sill replacement. Sill replacement is not difficult but it is the work required to ensure that the new sill is properly attached to sound metal that costs you money or time.

Sprites & Midgets

(Continued)

Frog Eye Sprites are not immune to attack from the front or rear. Accident damage to the one-piece wing and bonnet assembly is not easily mended and because there is no boot lid to alloy proper access, repairs to the rear panel and wings are also difficult. It is a good idea to stand directly behind the rear of the car as shown here and then move to the other side to compare the shape of the car — particularly around the rear lights. The bottom edge of the rear panel is rust prone and difficult to repair.

Never buy a Sprite or Midget without having looked carefully at the front floors, the entire floor edge and the rear bulkhead behind the seat backs. Avoid a car with patches over rotten metal. The cars with quarter elliptic rear springs are notorious for rusting and eventually breaking up around the rear bulkhead which is a heavily loaded area of the shell — problems in this area can be dangerous and are expensive to put right or a major task for the home restorer. I had thought that later cars with semi-elliptic rear springs did not suffer in this area but, as you can see from our

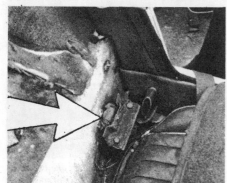

Outwardly this Sprite may look reasonable apart from the loss of the lower rear section of the wing, but look at the ground clearance and the gaping holes in the wheel arch and sill end just ahead of the rear wheel.

All the Sprites and Midgets share the same front suspension arrangement and the condition of the upper (indicated) and lower trunnions should be checked — advanced wear in the lower trunnion may mean that the lower wishbone has to be replaced. Handling is largely dependent on the condition of the front shock-absorbers and as a guide this can be checked by pressing down and then releasing the front of the car. If it feels soggy and the car tends to bounce they are due for replacement.

This is the same Sprite and the lack of ground clearance is explained by the forward spring mounting which has burst through the floor pan. It proves that all Sprites and Midgets, not just those with quarter elliptic rear springs, should be checked carefully in this area.

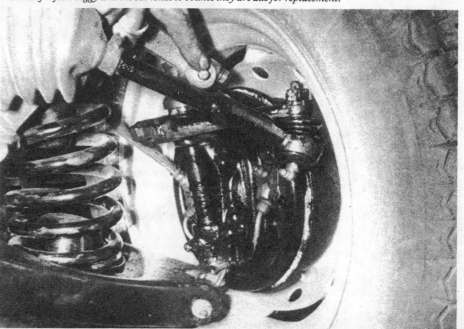

Early Sprites and Midgets had quarter elliptic rear springs which imposed considerable localised loadings on the shell at the rear of the floor pan. The wheel arch and lower edge of this car's wing looks dreadful — very poor repairs are common in these areas.

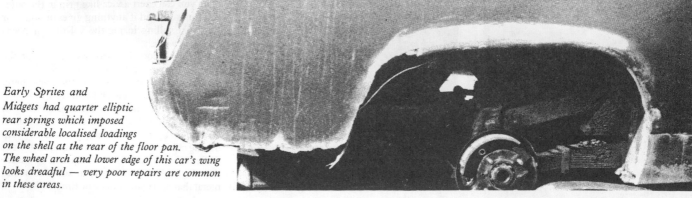

photographs, I was very much mistaken.

Rust around the rear wheel arches and at the bottom of the rear wings is a common failing and wing replacement is not so easy or cheap as you might expect, so look carefully for signs of all sorts of nasty repairs.

The bottom edges of doors on those cars with window glass, the lowest part of the boot lid and the leading edge of the bonnet on the post-Frog Eye cars are all water traps and panels are not as cheap as you may think. There are no new steel bonnets for Frog Eye Sprites and a fibreglass replacement lowers the value of the car. Repairing a steel Mk I Sprite bonnet is difficult or expensive, depending on who does the job, so check carefully for rust and accident damage. The rear wings of the

Mk I Sprite seem to suffer from minor knocks around the rear lights and you should compare the wings for shape.

The front suspension of the Sprite and Midget did not change throughout production (the 1500s excepted) and it is both simple and effective. Wear in the bottom trunnions should not be taken lightly and the condition of the dampers should be checked.

Wire wheels were fitted to some Sprites and Midgets and repairs or replacement can be

Engine access on the Mark I Sprite (Frog Eye) is exceptionally good, on the later cars it was still better than average. Engine life is generally good but an engine bay in this state does suggest some neglect. This is a 1,098 c.c. engine.

costly so inspect the condition of the spokes and look at the hub splines if you are serious about the car.

The engines are straightforward and have no real weaknesses to look out for — oil pressure, and, if you get the chance a compression test — will tell you a great deal about the condition of the engine. Gearbox whine is not at all uncommon, but a first and reverse gear that "chunters" or jumping out of gear indicates the need for a gearbox overhaul and may involve having to fit a 1,275 gearbox to the earlier cars with appropriate interchange of flywheel and engine back-plate.

While looking around the engine bay do look for signs of accident damage which might have affected the chassis legs. I once casually bought a "dead" Midget for rebuilding, failed to spot well disguised signs of repairs, and thought the car was surprisingly pleasant to drive. The truth came out when the engine

In direct contrast this is a very well cared for car with numerous improvements to its 1,275 c.c. engine which include a free-flow exhaust system, alloy rocker cover and electronic ignition. With the departure of the Sprite and Midget family, well-cared for examples like this will almost certainly steadily increase in value.

and gearbox were removed and the box would not come out of the tunnel — that car had been hit so hard that the tunnel was distorted and further checks showed that the wheel base was 1½ inches short on one side.

Trim and weather protection are reasonably hard wearing for what was a cheap car — if replacements are required it may not be so cheap a second time around.

On The Road

If possible, drive the car before coming to any final decision about buying a car that seems to meet your requirements. Even the 948cc cars make quite good use of the available power, but if the engine is tired it is a relatively cheap engine to replace or overhaul.

The steering of all the cars should be very good indeed and the brakes entirely adequate for normal road use. When I first arrived at a roundabout in damp conditions in a Sprite I was startled to find how easy it is to get the car sliding and any clumsy corrections make for very untidy progress — once you get the hang of the light, precise steering and accept that the grip on the road is not spectacularly good the handling is a joy, and very safe. If you get the Midget/Sprite bug other cars tend to feel clumsy and boring — the Mark I Sprite was intended to be cheap open air fun and a good example of any of the cars will still live up to that promise. □

The writer would like to thank those who assisted in producing this article, particularly Motobuild and John Sprinzel.

Two very different interiors — one which suggests the car is well cared for and one which would suggest a car which has suffered a lot of hard use and neglect which will not be cheap to put right. Both cars have non-standard steering wheels.

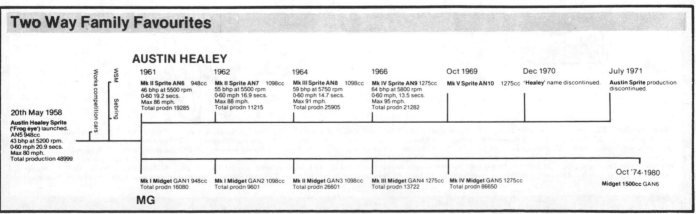

Two Way Family Favourites

AUSTIN HEALEY

20th May 1958
Austin Healey Sprite ('Frog eye') launched.
AN5 948cc
43 bhp at 5200 rpm.
0-60 mph 20.9 secs.
Max 80 mph.
Total production 48999

Works competition cars / WSM / Sebring

1961
Mk II Sprite AN6   948cc
46 bhp at 5500 rpm
0-60 19.2 secs.
Max 86 mph.
Total prodn 19285

1962
Mk II Sprite AN7   1098cc
55 bhp at 5500 rpm
0-60 mph 16.9 secs.
Max 88 mph.
Total prodn 11215

1964
Mk III Sprite AN8   1098cc
59 bhp at 5750 rpm
0-60 mph 14.7 secs.
Max 91 mph.
Total prodn 25905

1966
Mk IV Sprite AN9   1275cc
64 bhp at 5800 rpm
0-60 mph, 13.5 secs.
Max 95 mph.
Total prodn 21282

Oct 1969
Mk V Sprite AN10   1275cc

Dec 1970
'Healey' name discontinued.

July 1971
Austin Sprite production discontinued.

Mk I Midget GAN1 948cc
Total prodn 16080

Mk I Midget GAN2 1098cc
Total prodn 9601

Mk II Midget GAN3 1098cc
Total prodn 26601

Mk III Midget GAN4 1275cc
Total prodn 13722

Mk IV Midget GAN5 1275cc
Total prodn 86650

Oct '74-1980
Midget 1500cc GAN6

MG

'A' SERIES GEARBOX — THE PARTS

Exploded view of the later type of gearbox with needle roller bearings and baulk ring synchromesh

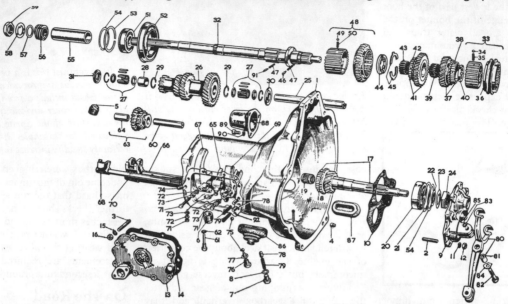

1 Gearbox bellhousing. 2 Stud for front cover. 3 Stud for side cover. 4 Dowel. 5 Filler plug. 6 Drain plug. 7 Plug for reverse plunger spring. 8 Washer. 9 Front cover. 10 Front cover joint. 11 Spring washer. 12 Nut. 13 Side cover. 14 Joint for side cover. 15 Spring washer. 16 Nut. 17 First motion shaft with cone. 18 Synchronising cone. 19 Needle roller bearing. 20 First motion shaft journal ball bearing. 21 Spring ring. 22 Washer. 23 Lockwasher. 24 Nut. 25 Layshaft. 26 Laygear. 27 Needle roller bearing with spring ring. 28 Distance piece. 29 Spring ring. 30 Thrust washer (front). 31 Thrust washer (rear). 32 Third motion shaft/mainshaft. 33 Third and fourth speed synchroniser. 34 Ball. 35 Spring. 36 Sleeve. 37 Third speed gear with cone. 38 Synchronising cone. 39 Needle roller. 40 Third speed gear locking collar. 41 Second speed gear with cone. 42 Synchronising cone. 43 Needle roller. 44 Splined locking washer. 45 Split washer. 46 Peg for locking collar. 47 Springs for pegs. 48 First speed gear assembly. 49 Ball. 50 Spring for ball. 51 Third motion shaft journal ball bearing. 52 Bearing housing. 53 Spring ring. 54 Bearing packing washer. 55 Third motion shaft distance piece. 56 Speedometer gear. 57 Plain washer. 58 Locking washer. 59 Third motion shaft nut. 60 Reverse gear shaft. 61 Locking screw. 62 Spring washer. 63 Reverse gear wheel and bush. 64 Bush. 65 Reverse fork. 66 Reverse fork rod. 67 First and second speed fork. 68 First and second speed fork rod. 69 Third and fourth speed fork. 70 Third and fourth speed fork rod. 71 Fork locating bolt. 72 Shakeproof washer. 73 Nut. 74 Interlock plunger. 75 Interlock ball. 76 Plug. 77 Washer. 78 Plunger for fork rod. 79 Spring. 80 Clutch withdrawal lever with bush. 81 Bush. 82 Bolt. 83 Spring washer. 84 Locking washer. 85 Nut. 86 Dust cover. 87 Dust cover for bell housing. 88 Starter pinion cover. 89 Screw. 90 Washer. 91 Spring loaded plunger.

Exploded view of the remote control components

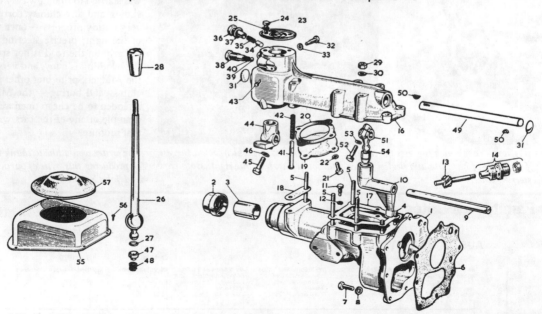

1 Rear extension. 2 Oil seal. 3 Sliding joint bush. 4 Extension short stud. 5 Extension long stud. 6 Joint. 7 Screw. 8 Spring washer. 9 Control shaft. 10 Control lever. 11 Control lever locating peg. 12 Spring washer. 13 Speedometer pinion. 14 Speedometer pinion oil seal assembly. 16 Remote control casing. 17 Extension front joing. 18 Extension rear joint. 19 Lever tower bottom cover. 20 Joint gasket. 21 Bolt. 22 Spring washer. 23 Lever seat cover. 24 Bolts. 25 Spring washer. 26 Change speed lever. 27 Ring (rubber). 28 Knob. 29 Stud nut. 30 Spring washer. 31 Welch plug. 32 Lever locating peg. 33 Spring washer. 34 Control shaft damper plunger. 35 Spring. 36 Spring retaining cap. 37 Washer. 38 Reverse selector detent plug. 39 Ball. 40 Spring. 41 Reverse selector plunger. 42 Spring. 43 Reverse selector plunger locating pin. 44 Rear selector lever. 45 Bolt. 46 Spring washer. 47 Thrust button. 48 Spring. 49 Remote control shaft. 50 Key. 51 Front selector lever. 52 Bolt. 53 Spring washer. 54 Front selector lever bush. 55 Remote control cover. 56 Screw. 57 Grommet.

Get Into Gear

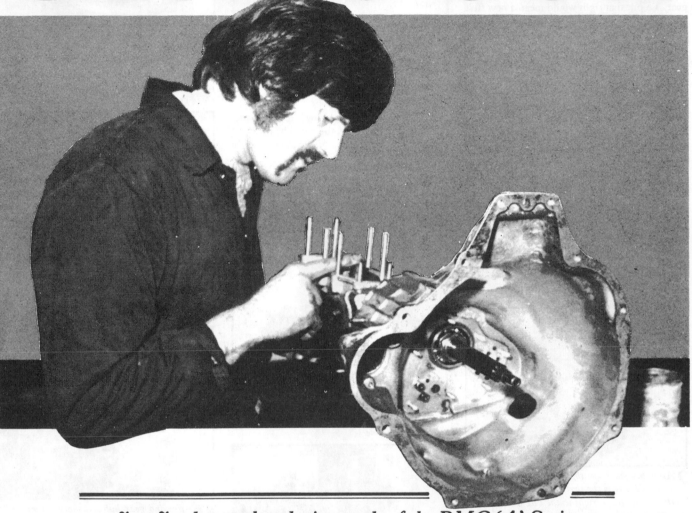

Joss Joselyn probes the internals of the BMC 'A' Series gearbox and shows that it is simpler than you might expect.

I once knew a chap who installed a clothes peg on the dashboard of his car. It was strategically placed so that when the gearlever was pushed into third, it slipped into the clothes peg and was held. There are, however, better ways of coping with a lever that jumps out of third and all the other potential gearbox troubles.

1 *Just to put into perspective the job you will be tackling, this array is the contents of a Sprite gearbox, the one just before it acquired synchromesh on first gear. Older boxes had cone synchromesh instead of the now more common baulk rings.*

To find out just what is possible and what is not a good idea, when it comes to the A-series box, I went down to *Hardy Engineering, 268 Kingston Road, Leatherhead, Surrey*. Here, it's a bit like Aladdin's cave, with racks of shiny new rebuilt boxes, stores full of bits, and a staff of engineers who know gearboxes inside out—which is the way they most often see them!

We decided that most people will find out how to take a gearbox to pieces but the most difficult aspects are going to be deciding what is worn and needs renewing, whether it is worth while or whether an exchange box would be cheaper and finally, the actual business of assembling the thing.

Dealing with the last of these first, assembly is shown photographically in our sequence, blow by painful blow. There's another group

of photographs showing what some typical forms of wear look like and I plan to go into the subject of cost in some detail.

Let's start at the beginning and think about what goes wrong with a gearbox to make you think it needs overhauling.

A common fault is bearings that rumble and it's possible, if problems are confined just to bearings, it could be worth while changing them. Prices are: front bearing — £6.40, rear bearing — £6.90, layshaft — £6.30, two layshaft bearings at 80p each, first motion shaft needle roller bearing £1.40. Now you'll probably need to fit three new baulk rings, at £4.60 each and you'll certainly need a new set of gaskets at £2. All that lot adds up to £38.40 and represents the minimum overhaul cost. If you want the work done professionally, it'll mean adding another £35 for labour—that's

Get Into Gear

what Hardy Engineering charge—which means a minimum price of £73.

Another common problem is a noisy first gear. To put that right would mean a new first /second hub assembly at £43 and a new laygear at £54. You'd certainly need gaskets and probably a bearing or two, so the total cost, doing all the work yourself, will be well over £100.

You can get a works reconditioned A-series gearbox for £110 on exchange and Hardy Engineering will do you one for £90—*need I say more?*

Jumping out of gear is another possibility and putting this right might just be worth while but only if the problems are in the selector forks and mechanism rather than in the engagement dogs. Directly you have to start renewing gears and their associated engagement dogs, the whole project becomes uneconomic.

For exactly the same reason, if you discover a chipped tooth on one of the gears, an

exchange box is the only economic solution; it means of course, not only fitting a new gear but also a new laygear and once you add on gaskets and possibly a bearing or two, you're well over the top and an exchange box is the only answer.

If we disregard the cold logic of economics for a moment, however, there will be plenty of people who, for reasons of their own, might

6 *Now the mainshaft is inverted in the vice so that third gear can be fitted. As with the second gear, a spring and plunger are inserted first and the carefully checked needle rollers are arranged in position, holding them with a film of clean grease.*

7 *The gear and synchronising cone go into position, lowering them carefully over the needle rollers. Now the spring-loaded plunger is pressed in while the third gear locking collar is pushed down and locked by turning.*

8 *First/second gear hub assembly comes next— another tricky operation. Two things have to be done; first, the plunger (arrowed in the photograph) has to be lined up with the flattened tooth in the hub outer; second, there are also three other balls and springs arranged around the hub inner which also have to be held in by the hub outer.*

want to take their gearbox apart and check its condition. The good news is that it is certainly possible and gearboxes don't really deserve the terrifying reputation they seem to have acquired. The problem seems to be that everyone manages to acquire some knowledge of engines but immediately panics at the thought of all those meshing gears, bearings, synchro hubs, dogs and what have you. But, as with engines, anything is possible provided you have the right information, the correct tools and a good bench to work on.

A prime essential is cleanliness—a clean bench, clean tools and plenty of clean rags and paraffin. Dismantling the thing under the car in the middle of a gravel drive is not to be recommended!

2 *Assembly starts on the mainshaft with second gear and here is the first step of all. The mainshaft is mounted upright in the vice and the little springs inserted as shown.*

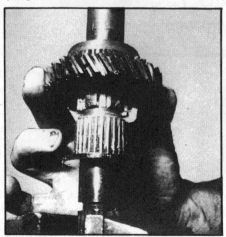

3 *The needle rollers are assembled in grease, taking great care to ensure they are all present, filling the space around the shaft. The plungers are inserted after the springs and the second gear and synchronising cone are then carefully lowered down over the needle roller assembly.*

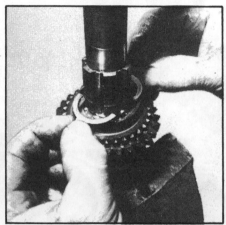

4 *Two keyed half washers are inserted next, ensuring they are properly seated in the synchronising cone.*

5 *Now comes the tricky bit. The splined locking washer has to be lowered down so that two cutouts on its underside locate over the tabs of the keyed half washers. The way that Hardy Engineering do this is to line the washer up first, as shown and then carefully mark the position of the front spring loaded plunger. A small 'nick' is then ground out so that the plunger can be depressed while the locking cap is lowered in position, after 'hooking' the rearmost plunger to hold it in. At the last minute the front plunger is released and rotating the cap will then allow the spring to reassert it, allowing it to lock internally.*

Our photographs show you primarily how to put the A-series box together but if you reverse the sequence, you'll get a good idea of how it all comes apart.

Releasing the selector forks from their rods is straightforward and, once this lot has gone and the cover is removed from the front of the box, the layshaft can be drifted out, knocking it from the rear end out into the bellhousing and allowing the laygear to fall into the bottom of the box.

The mainshaft comes next and, if the bearing housing sticks in the case as it might well do, find a suitable drift and tap it out from inside the gearbox.

Once this has gone, the circlip securing the first motion shaft on the bellhousing side can be taken out with circlip pliers and then the first motion shaft assembly tapped out by

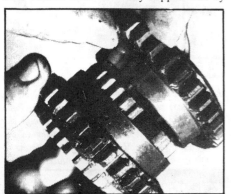

9 *Hardy Engineering line-up using an old hub outer the inside of which has been chamfered in the position where the three balls locate. This is comparatively easy to fit, the internal chamfers in the outer compressing the spring and recessing the balls as it is slid onto the hub inner. Then this is offered up to the hub inner that is being used, as shown in the photograph, once everything is lined up, a strong push on the hub inner moves it through the dummy outer and into the proper one, where the balls click into place.*

10 *Invert the mainshaft again so that 2nd gear is on top and onto the synchro cone; drop the 2nd gear synchro ring (baulk ring). Push down on it hard and make sure there is space underneath, as is being done here with that little probe. When it wears, it drops further down the cone, doesn't lock and that's when synchro problems start. Follow the synchro ring with the first/second gear hub assembly you have just built.*

11 *The mainshaft journal ball bearing comes next, together with its housing but check carefully for signs of pitting in the balls and particularly in the inner track.*

12 *Use a suitable diameter piece of tube as a drift to tap the bearing gently down into position.*

13 *Follow this with the distance piece, speedometer gear, plain washer, tab washer and main shaft nut.*

14 *Here the nut has just been tightened and the locking tab knocked over. If you use this method of tightening the nut, ensure that the splined shaft is gripped carefully at the position shown. This is clear of the part on which the propshaft slides but in any case, take great care to avoid damage.*

15 *Invert the shaft once again, this time so that third gear is on top. Drop the synchro ring (baulk ring) onto its cone and test there is a gap underneath and that it will lock up when twisted. Now drop the third/fourth hub assembly into position. This has the same three-ball arrangement when assembling as did the first/second gear hub.*

16 *The mainshaft is complete and attention is now turned to the first motion (spigot) shaft. On the left is the bare shaft, with the gear, dogs and synchroniser cone all an integral part. On the right the journal bearing has been added, followed by various washers and finally by a tab washer and nut.*

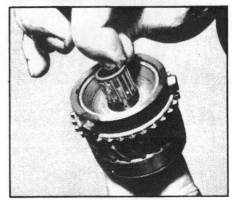

17 *Invert the first motion shaft and drop onto the synchroniser cone the fourth gear synchro ring (baulk ring). Then into the centre goes the little needle roller bearing. Now this assembly can be simply slipped onto the end of the mainshaft.*

striking the outer end until it falls out inside the box. The laygear can then be lifted out and the reverse idler freed by taking out the locking screw and pushing out the little shaft.

Keeping to the reverse order of the photographs, the gears, hubs, synchros, and all the other parts can be taken off their shafts, laying them out in the order in which they are removed. If it is not intended renewing the

Get Into Gear

(Continued)

18 Assembly of the gearbox proper can begin with the reverse idler. This is held in position inside the box while the shaft is slid through.

19 Turn the reverse idler shaft by means of a screwdriver in the end until holes in shaft and bearbox case line up and the locking screw can be tightened into position. Don't forget the spring washer.

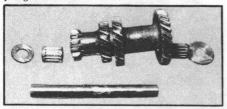

20 This is the laygear assembly, ready to go into the box. It is always a good idea to fit a new shaft but don't throw the old one away; you'll need it when reassembling.

21 Here is why; it is poked through at the back and used just to support the thrust washer. At the other end of the gearbox the same thing is done with the new layshaft and the other thrust washer.

22 The laygear goes into the box next, with its needle roller bearings ready inserted in each end, but it is simply laid in place and not fitted yet.

23 Now the mainshaft assembly is installed, being fed through and located until a few taps around the journal bearing housing locates it in its flange. Ensure the peg on the housing is at 10 o'clock and use the gasket to line it up exactly.

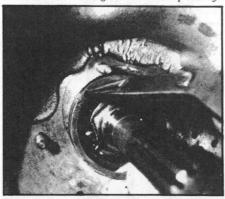

24 At the first motion shaft end, where it emerges into the bell housing, it is locked into position by means of a large circlip.

25 Using a large screwdriver, inserted through the side aperture, lift the laygear cluster until it meshes with the gears on the mainshaft and then push the layshaft through from the front end. Feed it carefully into the thrust washer and housing in the back of the box, pushing out the old shaft which had been used as a temporary support for the washer.

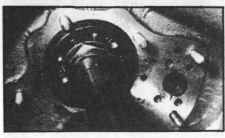

26 Ensure the layshaft key is at the angle shown.

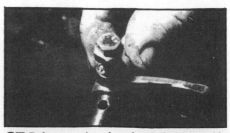

27 Before starting the selector fork assembly, try the reverse selector fork on its rod and adjust the locking screw until it just slides but will catch in the hole in the rod. Then slide it off again.

28 Fit the reverse selector fork in position on reverse gear and enter the selector rod through the casing and just into the fork. Now fit 3rd/4th gear selector fork on its coupling sleeve and pass the reverse gear selector rod through the clearance hole in it and into its housing in the front end of the box. Locate the locking screw in its hole in the rod and tighten it in place.

29 This is the 3rd/4th selector rod in position and this does go in next but before it is inserted into its housing at the front end, a ball, shown here on the end of a screwdriver is inserted, so that it is positioned inside the casing between the reverse selector rod and the 3rd/4th selector rod. A second ball goes in at this front end to interlock between the 3rd/4th gear selector rod and the 1st/2nd gear selector rod.

30 An alternative way of inserting these is by removing these plugs. If you remove them, fit new fibre washers under the heads.

31 At the back of the box, insert an interlock slug, as shown, to interlock 1st/2nd gear selector rod against reverse.

Some Examples of Wear

A1 *A well-chewed example of square-cut teeth (first gear) on a lay gear cluster, contrasted on the left with a new example.*

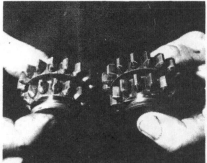

A2 *Another nasty example of wear. This is the reverse idler and the one on the left is well-worn.*

A3 *It's not always the gear teeth that go; the end of the mainshaft is the bit that fits inside a little needle roller bearing in the first motion shaft can suffer too, as witness the one on the left compared with a new example.*

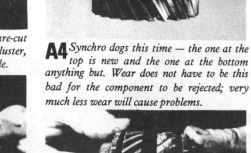

A4 *Synchro dogs this time — the one at the top is new and the one at the bottom anything but. Wear does not have to be this bad for the component to be rejected; very much less wear will cause problems.*

A5 *No need for comment here — those helical teeth are well graunched!*

A6 *More chewed up teeth — this time on the first/second gear hub.*

34 *The front cover can be refitted next, installing a new gasket, refitting original shims, and ensuring that the half-moon projection on the end of the layshaft is at the right angle to match the half-moon in the cover.*

35 *At the rear end, another gasket goes in place and then the gearbox rear extension is fitted, ensuring that the selector striker engages in the rods. Insert the securing bolts with their washers and nuts.*

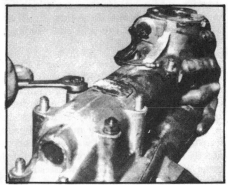

36 *Another gasket and then the remote control housing can be installed on its studs and the nuts tightened down.*

Rebuilding

Ensure every component is clean before assembling it. A paraffin bath is probably the best way to clean, using an old paint brush to ensure every crevice is spotless. Use clean grease to assemble needle rollers and use clean gearbox oil on all the other parts as they are assembled.

A new layshaft is always a good idea and it is just as well to fit new thrust washers as well.

A useful tip, before fitting the mainshaft, is to heat the casing. This enables the bearing housing to be moved easily to line up the peg exactly.

Don't try to re-use old gaskets; a new set will ensure there are no oil leaks when the job is finished.

One last important check—before you put the gearbox back in the car, refit the gearlever and just ensure it changes smoothly into each gear. Better safe than sorry! □

(lower left)

32 *Now the 1st/2nd gear selector rod can go into position, passing it through the top hole in the casing and locking it into its selector fork.*

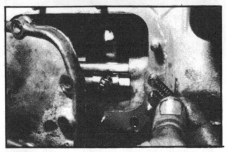

33 *Two more plungers are inserted, rounded ends first, into holes in the front edge of the side cover and these are followed by two springs. The cover is then fitted with a new gasket and secured in position with eight nuts.*

first/second or third/fourth gear hub assembly, there is no point in dismantling it unless the balls and springs holding the two together need changing. If taking them apart can be avoided, it will save a lot of problems putting them back together again; no one at home is likely to have the spare specially-ground hub outer that Hardy Engineering use!

Bearing wear is usually fairly obvious. In the large journal ball bearings it will show up as scoring or pitting in the balls themselves and

in the outer track. If the box has done a high mileage, they will almost certainly need renewal in any case.

The little needle rollers can also be pitted and, in the case of the bearing on the end of the mainshaft, where the load is heavy, the bearing may well have broken up and damaged the journal on the end of the shaft.

A selection of other types of wear can be seen in the separate group of photographs.

Prize Sprite

Our choice of an Austin-Healey Sprite as the prize for our competition was a carefully considered one — we think it is a car with character, is easy to maintain by the home handyman (or lady!), and is historically significant as the first of the most successful line of small sports cars ever made. In other words, the Sprite can claim to be the epitomy of the affordable classic car.

The Austin-Healey '100' had already been in production for three or four years when, in 1956, Donald Healey and Len Lord of Austin first discussed the possibility of making a baby sports car — a 'bug' as Sir Leonard described it. He mainly wanted it to sell in North America, where his dealers were asking for something a little less hairy than the '100' which they could sell to sons and daughters rather than mums and dads.

So Donald Healey returned to his Warwick factory and, with son Geoff Healey, chassis designer Barry Bilbie, and body draughtsman Gerry Coker, set to work creating a small sports car out of Austin parts; and it was the A35 from which most of the mechanical parts were borrowed, although it was found that the Morris Minor rack and pinion steering fitted better, so this was incorporated instead of the A35's steering box.

The Austin-Healey Sprite thus emerged with the A35's free-revving 948cc 'A' series engine and coil-spring/wishbone front suspension, though at the back was a fairly unusual cantilever arrangement for the 'live' rear axle, which was suspended by quarter-elliptic springs from the car's rear bulkhead. The body shell was assembled by John Thompson Motor Pressings, and the famous 'frog-eye' headlights came about after a pop-up system proved to be too expensive for production. It was made at Austin's Longbridge plant and was an immediate success — some 50,000 were made between 1958 and 1961, when it was replaced by the Mk II Sprite with its conventional bonnet.

Even in the late 'fifties, the original Sprite wasn't exactly fast — nippy is a better description. After all, the A35 engine merely had twin carburettors added, raising the bhp from 34 to 42 and allowing the car to just about reach 80mph; but it was extremely manoeuvrable and could surprise much bigger cars down a twisty road.

The editor and Terry begin the process of removing the Sprite's bonnet.

'OUR' SPRITE

Well, for the time being it is — soon it could be yours! We took some months to locate what we thought was the 'right' car, which we envisaged as being an original example but (to use that time-honoured phrase), 'in need of some work'. We purposely avoided looking at cars which had been recently rebuilt, because unless you *know* how the work has been done first-hand, you can end up paying for someone else's bodging; but on the other hand, we didn't want a 'heap' which could possibly take months to put right.

We found what seemed to be a promising car advertised in 'Exchange & Mart', and Michael Brisby went straight across to St. John's Wood to view it. The decision to buy was made almost instantly — 255 JPH had been owned by a professional musician for five years so all its recent history was known, it was as original as you could hope for (down to the original 948cc engine), and its state of preservation seemed far above average —

crowned by the straightest, most rust-free bonnet Michael and I had ever seen on an unrestored Frog (and if you didn't know, the large, wings-and-bonnet assembly is a highly prized item amongst Sprite enthusiasts if in good condition — many cars have had glass fibre substitutes fitted).

Within days the car was at our Worcester workshop — we decided to bring the car up to scratch ourselves rather than place it with a specialist (not that there *are* very many Sprite rebuild specialists yet!) because there is nothing like 'doing it yourself'. Anybody with the money can take it to a professional restorer and just watch, but we like to practice what we preach wherever possible, and this way you, the reader, learn more.

So Michael and I climbed into our well-worn overalls and, with Terry of 'Terry's Tips' fame, began the stripping-out process, having noted any missing items; basically this meant disconnecting the battery and then removing the bonnet, seats and what little interior trim there is in a Sprite. The actual

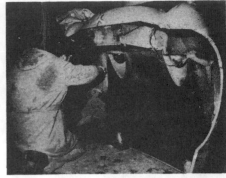

Close examination of the detached bonnet confirmed our expectations of its excellent condition — virtually no rust at all and only a couple of repaired dents. We can hardly believe that it has been on the car since new and reckon its age to be more like five years, which is when the car was last resprayed. ▲

Editor Michael Brisby and Terry Bramhall (of 'Terry's Tips') confer over the condition of our 'prize Sprite' after removing the interior trim, and compile a shopping list to take to A.H. Spares.
◀

story of what we found and how we tackled it will be retold in subsequent issues, but meanwhile we can say that we're very pleased with the car and, while we are not attempting to produce a 'concours' Sprite, it is going to turn out very, very well. Filled in your entry form yet? □

Frog-spawn; hundreds of Sprites awaiting export at Longbridge. New, they cost £678.17s.0d — but that was 21 inflationary years ago.

Rebuilding our Prize Sprite

We continue the story of how we produced a Sprite fit for a winner.

Besides representing a valuable prize for our competition, 255 JPH has also provided us with a highly interesting and rather thorough rebuild story — because much as we expected, an awful lot needed doing once we began to take the car apart. Up until recently, not many people have taken the trouble to restore Sprite bodywork seriously, mainly because the value of the car didn't justify it, but this is changing and Frog-eye restoration is becoming something of a national sport. So if you're thinking about tackling such a job, read on!

CONSTRUCTION

First of all it's essential to know how the Sprite was put together in the first place. It is built in three major parts — the floor/bulkheads assembly, rear outer bodywork, and the bonnet. The former is the most important as takes most of the road stresses. It's composed of a flat floor with an integral transmission tunnel flanked by two hollow chassis rails which end at a hollow cross-member under the seats. The tunnel is continued to a double-thickness rear bulkhead into which is built compartments on each side which carry the mountings for the cantilevered rear springs. At the front, the longitudinal chassis members continue under an integral welded-up front bulkhead, and either side of the engine, flanked by welded-on inner wings.

This whole assembly was built by John Thomson Motor Pressings of Wolverhampton from some 50 pieces ranging in thickness from 21 SWG to 1/8ins plate. It was then delivered to Pressed Steel at Swindon where the rear inner wings, boot floor, and rear outer panels were assembled on it. Outer sills, scuttle panels and doors followed. Finally, the front wings and bonnet assembly, which hinges up in one piece from the bulkhead, was added.

Although there are no rear spring hangers to worry about, it is because of this that the rear bulkhead is of vital concern, as it provides the only mounting point for the projecting quarter-elliptic rear springs, and is therefore subject to a lot of localised stress. Unfortunately, many would-be repairers don't seem to appreciate this fact and just carry out some cosmetic plating of the area which would resist the prod of an MoT inspector's screwdriver (if they are allowed even that) but little else. Eventually the whole lot will give way, the body will drop, and the spring will protrude violently into the passenger compartment. If this were to happen at speed the results are better imagined than experienced.

Our car had suffered most of the common bodges even though by absolute standards it remained an original, much above average example; it appeared to have undergone an extensive body 'overhaul' about five years ago (the last owner before us had the car for about that long) and our strip-down revealed some quite amazing handiwork using cigar tins, bits of aluminium, and lots of glass fibre. The story is told in the pictures:

Rebuilding our Prize Sprite

Our first job on beginning the Sprite revival was to remove the battery and then the petrol tank, which is secured by six studs to the underside of the boot floor. These came undone okay, but in the end we had to give up unscrewing the petrol union and cut the line. Tank was drained first, but even then there is a serious risk of fire or explosion; Terry holds an extinguisher while the Editor pulls the tank clear. It was stored carefully out of harm's way.

Next came the interior trim (what there is of it in a Sprite!) and the seats; some of the bolts securing the runners proved difficult to remove and no wonder, when we finally attacked the floor itself! Plates had been bolted and pop rivetted to the floor and the whole covered with a thick glass fibre mat . . .

. . . which we pulled away complete on each side to end up with crude Sprite floor 'mouldings', displayed here by Terry rather like fishing trophies!

Under the 'mat' the remains of the original floor had been covered by plates like this one; note bolt holes.

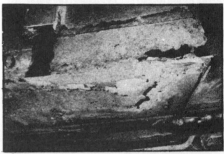

The offside outer sill was glass fibre and when removed, disclosed a very rotten inner sill and footwell, the latter covered inside the car by a 'new' floor of galvanised steel just placed over the top and glued in at the edges by filler. This is a view looking up from underneath, just behind the front wheel.

Door pillar on the driver's side looked dodgy, and appeared to be coming detached at the bottom; check-strap was broken too, with consequences that would become apparant later.

We weren't far wrong — the door hinge pillar was covered by what appeared to be a bit of aluminium from a bus platform, instead of the steel outer shroud panel which should have been there and which had probably suffered from the door swinging wide open.

Then we took a look at the all-important rear spring mounting area. Typically, the outer box section of the rear bulkhead had been covered by a pop-rivetted sheet of aluminium inside the rear wheel arch . . .

The next step here was to carefully remove the rusty metal, having first removed the bolts securing the forward part of the bottom spring mounting plate.

This plate can better be seen looking upwards from underneath; the road spring is secured to it by 'U' bolts. Fortunately for us, on this car the heavier-gauge steel box actually containing the spring was sound, so it was a question of repairing around it. On other Sprite's we've done, the whole spring assembly has had to be removed entirely and the inner box sections reconstructed as well.

. . . which on removal disclosed the equally typical rot which had virtually disposed of the metal making up this section altogether.

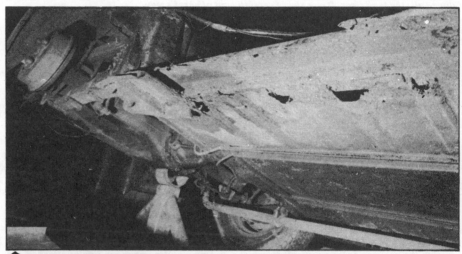

The same area, viewed from inside the car. At the bottom, a piece of steel had been bolted through the remains of the outer floor and pop-rivetted to the vertical face of the bulkhead, providing no structural support whatsoever. The discarded plate can be seen bottom right.

We had hoped to finish our repairs to the floor at the point where the longitudinal strengthener ran back to the bulkhead, but as can be seen, both this and the floor some inches inwards of it had suffered too badly to be used. Note that at this stage the car is supported so that the shell is stressed as if it was on its wheels — lifting the car at one side will twist the whole structure.

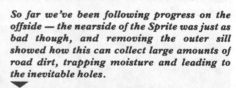

So far we've been following progress on the offside — the nearside of the Sprite was just as bad though, and removing the outer sill showed how this can collect large amounts of road dirt, trapping moisture and leading to the inevitable holes.

Rebuilding our Prize Sprite

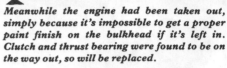

Meanwhile the engine had been taken out, simply because it's impossible to get a proper paint finish on the bulkhead if it's left in. Clutch and thrust bearing were found to be on the way out, so will be replaced.

Similarly, the nearside floors were cut back to sound metal — Terry holds the sorry remains. Note that the longitudinal strengthener box which runs from front (jacking point) cross member to the rear bulkhead has been removed as well.

The area around the jacking point was left, complete with section of inner sill. This is essential, in order to leave a reference point for when the new inner sill is offered up. New steel floor sections have been made up and laid in place as can be seen.

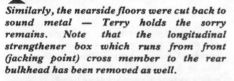

Another task which was undertaken during the body repairs was to strip all the paintwork off the body, which included the excellent steel bonnet. Cleaned up, the car will have been painted by the time you read this, by Cottons of Worcester — Volvo agents but (thanks to TR and Healey enthusiast Tony Matthews who's manager) with both a soft spot for 'classics' and a knowledge of the standard of finish required on a car which is to be a competition prize!

New outer sills were obtained from AH Spares of Leamington Spa, who adapt the current BL Midget item by letting-in the Frog's jacking point hole, and filling in unwanted badge clip holes. They also sell inner sills, but as these are merely flat pieces of sheet steel, we elected to make them ourselves, cutting the necessary holes and slots as shown.

Here the new inner sill is offered up to the Sprite floor pan to check dimensions. Hinge pillar has yet to be repaired.

Next month, we'll be concluding the Sprite rebuild by showing you exactly how all the new metal was fitted to floor, rear bulkhead, and door pillars. We'll also be seeing how the car was sprayed by a professional to a very high standard, thanks to Cottons of Worcester who've gained at least one "Best Paint" award at a major national 'concours' before now. Unless you are very patient and have lots of time we reckon that the final paint job after an extensive rebuild should be carried out under controlled conditions by an expert. It is, after all, what everyone sees and we've seen a number of good rebuilds spoilt by an indifferent respray. □

Rebuilding our Prize Sprite

The end comes in sight!

Not that stripping down to bare metal makes it entirely easy for the painter, because this usually reveals a large number of minor imperfections in the metal itself, formerly covered with paint and/or plastic filler. These have to be tackled individually during the priming stages using stopper, though modern 'primer-fillers' cope well with small defects straight from the gun. How long is devoted to this sort of preparation governs both the cost and the eventual quality of the job.

We wanted a good, respectable paint job from Cottons in line with our aim to produce a good, usable Frog-eye Sprite for our lucky winner. What we've got is a full-blown 'concours' paint finish which wouldn't disgrace a national show car! I suppose we shouldn't be too surprised, as Tony Matthews' own cars (TR3A and Healey 3000) were both painted at Cottons and both have won shelves-full of 'concours' awards. We just hope the new owner will appreciate what he's got — and will look after it!

Bulkhead was repaired by making up two new pieces and welding in — taking care not to overheat dash wiring behind, although this was to be renewed. After grinding back the welds, minor blemishes were filled.

Ah well, the best-laid plans of mice and men... We'd hoped to have our 'prize Sprite' all finished and ready to go by the time this issue went to press, but the rebuild conformed to the usual pattern for such things and got behind schedule. So we can't quite show you the completed car, but can only go as far as the painting of the shell.

What we can do though is, go over a few items which we left out of previous instalments — the repair of a battery acid hole in the bulkhead, and the rear wing repair that was needed after a large chunk of glass fibre was removed from the offside. These are detailed in the pictures.

Returning to the paintwork, this was carried out in a professional workshop — we'll be respraying an entire car ourselves with the Apollo 'hot air' sprayer featured in this month's competition another time, but home resprays are usually lengthy exercises and for the Sprite, we needed an excellent job done relatively quickly. Luckily, Worcester Volvo agents Cottons agreed to do the job, and we presented them with the repaired shell, rubbed down to bare metal.

This way of doing things is worth remembering if you're involved in a rebuild — if you're not confident about respraying a car yourself but want a high-quality finish, the desired results can be acheived at moderate cost by preparing the car entirely yourself and delivering it to the professional spray shop. You can then pick it up and take it home to fit up yourself, paying only for the paint and spraying time. The only sure way to arrive at a good,

lasting finish on an older car is, to our way of thinking, to strip to bare metal because otherwise it's almost impossible to predict what sort of reaction you're going to get when spraying over old paint, even if a heavy sealer-coat is applied first — all too often the old finish can bleed through a few weeks after, or erupt with craters, pimples or crazing.

Stripping of the bulkhead revealed holes caused by battery acid. Note that the heater duct has been masked to stop any debris entering and you must take great care with the temperature gauge pipe seen lying on top of the scuttle.

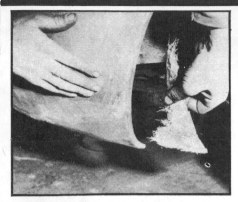

Bottom corner of offside rear wing was found to have a complete 'glass' section under the paint. New section was shaped and welded in place, and afterwards lead filled.

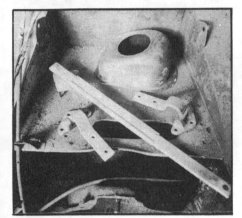

Bodywork was completely stripped to bare metal, and small items sandblasted — a process which gives results almost impossible to duplicate by hand because it gets in every crevice.

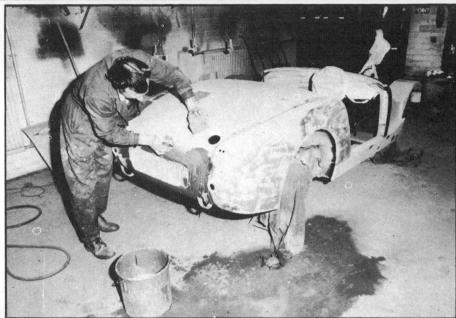

Car was then handed over to Cottons, where Jim is seen rubbing-down an application of stopper — this process was carried out three or four times. Wing shows how guide coat has been sanded back, showing where the high-spots and troughs are, to be made good with more stopping.

Jim applies the 'Cherry Red' cellulose. Note method of suspending loom out of the way — we hadn't then decided to completely rewire so left it on car.
Note method of suspending loom out of the way — we hadn't then decided to completely rewire so left it on car.

The quality of the paint finish means that we are having to take even greater pains to reassemble the Sprite to a similar standard; with that finish under the bonnet, we could hardly bolt back a beaten-up old heater box and tatty electrical gear, so more work has gone into detail finishing then perhaps we'd anticipated. If you're building a true concours car, this type of attention is absolutely essential and poor detailing will let down even the best panel and paintwork — after all, it's what everybody sees. Minor bracketry and so on was sand-blasted (there's probably someone in your area who can take this on, and it saves a vast amount of tedious scraping), while the wiring (which was dubious anyway) was tackled by getting a new loom from Autosparks of Hull. Other small fixtures (grommets, clips, badges etc) were obtained from Moto-build or AH Spares.

As we write this, the Sprite is still at Cottons because Terry agreed with Tony Matthews that the new paint should be given at least two or three days to harden before everything was bolted back — trying to hurry the procedure would only cost time later on in repairing fingermarks and scratches. International Healey Day at Ashton Court, where the car will be handed over, is only three weeks off, but we're confident we can finish it in time. We think.

Just as much attention had been paid to the surface finish on the bulkhead and under-bonnet areas, seen here receiving the colour coat. Pictures of finished car next month!

So, a 'final' final instalment next month after all. But we've enjoyed the task of bringing this little 1959 sports car up to scratch and hope that the project has given other owners some encouragement, because while the Sprite does have its tricky points, we think it *is* a car that virtually anyone could rebuild at home, given patience, a minimum of equipment — and a regular order for *'Practical Classics'!* ☐

GOODBYE TO OUR SPRITE

On Sunday, July 6th at International Healey Day, a very smart Frog-eye Sprite with gleaming cherry-red paintwork was handed over to a delighted new owner. The car was, of course, the first prize in our 'Win A Sprite' competition, and just four months previously had been virtually nothing more than a pile of dirty, rusty bits and pieces. Regular readers will have seen how it came back to life step-by-step, and now that we have said good-bye to our first project, we can conclude the story with this final instalment.

We left the Sprite in mid-respray last month, just before a slight drama had occured! Jim Barnes, Cottons' painter, had sprayed the final coat of red when general manager Tony Matthews came into the spray shop one morning and suddenly realised that it was the wrong shade... Great consternation all round, and we came down to look at the car ourselves — sure enough, instead of a bright cherry red, there was a sort of rust-colour tinge in the paintwork; an investigation revealed that an additional tin of paint ordered hadn't been mixed up to the correct specification. But none of us could face letting the car go with that non-original tint, so poor Jim had to re-finish the entire car with the correct red.

This left only just over two weeks before International Healey Day so while the paint hardened, we commenced the re-fit at Cottons; the front suspension was given new kingpins and lower fulcrum pins, and refitted complete

with new coil springs, which counteracted the front-end sag noticeable before. Then we took the car away to install the engine, complete with its new clutch and timing chains — precautionary measures while everything was accessible.

Next, the brakes were overhauled using 'Handy' copper brake piping which we found easy to use (and it looks good too, besides being much safer than the original rust-prone steel piping), replacing the rear wheel cylinders at the same time as they were somewhat pitted (in fact they didn't look as if they'd worked for a considerable period).

These rear cylinders are as for Morris Minors of the same period, incidentally. A snag cropped up in the form of a worn handbrake compensator (see picture), and as a replacement was not immediately available, we drilled and re-tapped the block and replaced the equally worn threaded stud which screws into it with a bolt cut to a suitable length (the old stud was removed by cutting the welds which secured it).

Meanwhile, the new loom from Autosparks of Hull was fitted, which we found quite easy thanks to it being a quality product with all the right colour codings; all we had to do was alter a few connectors (i.e. spade to screw-in type). Then because of the superb finish Cottons had achieved on the underbonnet and bulkhead areas, we decided to replace a few electrical items with ones in better condition — Terry found a new-looking fuse box with the correct screw-type terminals on a scrap P4 Rover and a control box from a late-fifties Hillman, while AH Spares sold us a brand new starter switch.

Other components were just well-cleaned, metal-finish items being buffed-up on a wire wheel (it's amazing the finish you can get using a bench-mounted electric grinding wheel), including nuts and bolts (which are expensive to replace anyway, these days!). We located a 'new' rocker box with the correct metal oil-filler cap, while from the same scrap-yard came a period cast heater stop-cock which was suitably cleaned up — this came from an A30, a car which with the A35 represents a very good source of period oddments for a Mk I or II Sprite. A choke cable and knob to very nearly original spec. came from a Mk I A40 Farina (just a 4-ins outer sleeve extension had

The engine bay of the finished Sprite, complete and gleaming; about the only missing item is the trunking to the heater, which we hope to supply later.

Re-upholstered and re-carpeted interior of the Sprite, with original wheel courtesy of Motobuild — quite a rare item these days.

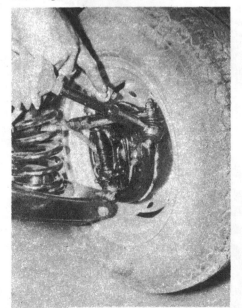

Front suspension was attended to as necessary, with an overhauled upright.

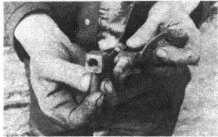

Handbrake compensator block was worn oval, and had to be re-drilled and tapped; worn stud was replaced by suitably shortened bolt.

Rust-proofing after the body rebuild was an essential — Paul Skilleter treats the sills and jacking points with Tectyl; old (original) metal was treated with Waxoyl.

Original-type jacking point covers are from A40 floor well!

to be added to make it operate on the Sprite), while we found that an elderly MGB dash supplied a correctly shaped knob for the push/pull heater switch — a minute's work with a fine-tipped soldering iron produced the requisite 'H' marking. The gear-lever rubber gaiter is as for Mk I A40, while the same car yields jacking-point rubber covers in mint condition — they're used on the A40 to cover the rear shock absorber access holes in the floor pan!

Originally the Sprite had moulded rubber floor coverings but these seem totally non-obtainable as one would expect, so like most other owners we used carpets. The seats had previously been restored using covers supplied by Gerry Sailes (see last month's Going Spare) — as he advises, do one seat at a time so you have a pattern to refer to, and ensure that sharp edges on the seat frames are padded to avoid tearing. The dash was re-covered in similar red vinyl too (note that this material covers a small access hole for an electrician's screwdriver which is the only way to get at the screw which holds the ignition switch in).

With the various chrome fixtures in place, the car really did begin to look good, and while

we intended merely to produce a healthy, usable Sprite for our winner, we think he's ended up with something a little better than just that. Not that we consider 255 JPH to be a true 'concours' car — it would require many more hours than we could economically devote to the project to produce that sort of vehicle; in fact, the work (excluding paint but including fitting-up and all mechanical tasks) extended to some 550 hours all told, though ideally we would have preferred to have spent a little longer playing with the bonnet fit, and the doors. Thereby hangs a tale, incidentally, not to mention a moral — we'd achieved an excellent door fit with all shoulders level but omitted to tell the paintshop that the hinges had been carefully selected and matched to arrive at this; so when they took the doors off to paint the door jams etc., needless to say the hinges got muddled up and we lost our excellent fit . . . and with the car fully painted there was little we could do about it. Next time we'll either paint those parts of the doors ourselves, or arrive at a numbering system for the hinges.

PC Editor Michael Brisby hands over the Sprite's documents to winner Richard Robinson at International Healey Day.

The Sprite's lucky new owner prepares to drive back home to Reading with his prize. Watch out for it!

Rebuilding the 'prize Sprite' has been great fun, if hard work. We enjoyed it, and we hope that you the reader have learnt something about putting one of these small sports cars to rights, and about restoration work in general. The new owner, Richard Robinson, says he intends to keep the car, so look out for it at Austin-Healey Club events and give it our regards; we shall miss its cheeky presence in our workshop. □